PRAISE FOR
77 Reasons Why Your Book Was Rejected

"There's a lot of straight dope in these pages. Mike Nappa cuts through a lot of how-to fluff to give writers some inside info on what makes editors say no and what makes them say yes."

—Chuck Sambuchino, Editor, *Guide to Literary Agents* and
Children's Writer's & Illustrator's Market

"This is a great, practical book for those seeking publication in today's market. *77 Reasons Why Your Book Was Rejected* is jammed with good, workable ideas to help every potential author."

—Chip MacGregor, President of MacGregor Literary and former
VP/Publisher at Time Warner (Hachette Book Group USA)

"*77 Reasons Why Your Book Was Rejected* is a must-read book for writers who want to get their book in print. Not only will you learn why your manuscript has been rejected, you'll learn how to fix it. Mike Nappa draws from a wealth of publishing experience and tells it like it is. You may not always like what he says; but if you do what he says, you'll be a step closer to publication."

—Marlene Bagnull, Director, Colorado and Greater Philadelphia
Christian Writers Conferences

"In this book, Mike Nappa lists every conceivable reason why a publisher would reject your book as well as sage advice on what to do about it. Invaluable for both novice and experienced authors alike."

—Robert Bly, America's Top Copywriter, and author of
88 Money-Making Writing Jobs and
Careers for Writers

77 REASONS Why *Your Book Was* REJECTED

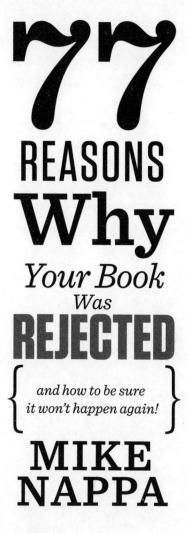

{ *and how to be sure it won't happen again!* }

MIKE NAPPA

 sourcebooks

Published by Sourcebooks, Inc.
P.O. Box 4410, Naperville, Illinois 60567-4410
(630) 961-3900
Fax: (630) 961-2168
www.sourcebooks.com

Library of Congress Cataloging-in-Publication Data

Nappa, Mike
  77 reasons why your book was rejected (and how to be sure it won't happen again!) / Mike Nappa.
    p. cm.
  Includes bibliographical references.
  1. Authorship–Marketing–Handbooks, manuals, etc. 2. Authors and publishers–Handbooks, manuals, etc. 3. Book proposals. I. Title. II. Title: Seventy-seven reasons why your book was rejected (and how to be sure it won't happen again!).
  PN161.N37 2011
  808'.02–dc23

                                    2011017363

          Printed and bound in the United States of America.
                  VP 10 9 8 7 6 5 4 3 2 1

Obstacles don't have to stop you. If you run into a wall, don't turn around and give up. Figure out how to climb it, go through it, or work around it.

—Michael Jordan,
in *I Can't Accept Not Trying*

{ Contents }

{ Introduction }

It Takes Less Than a Minute to Reject Your Book

I make it my goal to reject every book proposal you send me in sixty seconds or less.

This includes book ideas that come in my email box, that are hand-delivered to me at a writer's conference, that are recommended by a friend of a friend who knew somebody who told them I was in the publishing business, or whatever. If you've got a book you want to publish, and you send it to me, chances are very good that I will reject your proposal in under a minute.

The sad part about this goal of mine is that it's remarkably easy to accomplish. Too easy, in fact. Over the last two-plus decades, I've worked as an acquisitions editor for three publishers and also as the founder and chief literary agent of Nappaland Literary Agency. I regretfully admit to you now that in that time I've issued thousands and thousands of those hated rejection letters, in all shapes and forms, to well-meaning and talented writers just like you.

I've looked an eager author in the eye and said, "I'm sorry, but I'm not interested in publishing your book." I've sent countless emails, several variations on form letters, and even experimented with that stupid "checklist" rejection where a dozen reasons for declining are listed on the page and all I have to do is put an X next to my favorite insult for you. ("Your book doesn't meet our quality standards," "We are not able to project a significant interest for your book," and so on.)

Now, before you label me as some sort of sadist toward the struggling masses of writers out there, you should also know that I am an author myself. In fact, I've published (as author or co-author) more than forty books, sold more than a million copies of those books, won awards, been translated into various foreign languages, and all kinds of good stuff like that.

What that really means is this:

- In my career, I've happily received forty-plus acceptance letters or phone calls about my book ideas. (Yay me!)
- At the same time, by my best estimates, I've also personally received *more than 2,000 rejections* for my book ideas. (Ouch!)

And yes, I've had to sit stone-faced while some arrogant jerk of an editor looked me dead in the eye and said, "I'm sorry, but I'm not interested in publishing your book." I've received countless emails, several variations on form letters, and even some of those stupid "checklist" rejections where a dozen reasons for declining are listed on the page and all the contemptuous editor had to do was put an X next to her favorite insult for me.

So, you could say that for the past few decades I've been a successful author, editor, and literary agent. And you could also say during that time I've *successfully failed* at being an author, editor, and literary agent.

And that's what this book is about. Learning why we fail—and then turning that knowledge into success the next time around.

I think Craig Ferguson, host of the *Late Late Show* on CBS, sums it up best. "We prepare for glory," he says, "by failing until we don't."[1] That rings true in the life of a professional writer. Still, failure by itself is of no benefit. It's just another disappointing circumstance in life. However, failure with knowledge gained…well, that's something completely different.

So, with that (and you) in mind, I've culled more than twenty years of my experience as a publishing industry professional and compiled it for you here, boiled down to *77 Reasons Why Your Book Was Rejected (and how to be sure it won't happen again!)*. It's my hope that you'll find this little tome insightful, helpful, and most of all, something that will give you what you need to get past your last rejection and move on to your rightful place of book publishing glory.

HOW TO USE THIS BOOK

I'll be wearing both my "acquisitions editor" and "literary agent" caps while we chat in the pages here. So if I say something like,

---

1 Craig Ferguson, *American on Purpose* (New York: Harper, 2009), xiii.

"When you send me your proposal…," you can assume that "me" in that sentence refers to both "me-the-generic-acquisitions-editor" and "me-the-generic-literary-agent." I'm making myself your stand-in for those roles. If something is editor-specific or agent-specific, I'll let you know. For instance, if I say something like, "When I bring this to my VP of sales…," that'll mean I'm obviously talking from inside the publishing house—wearing the editorial hat. When I mention something like, "As I create my pitch list for this book…," that's clearly me operating outside the publishing house—wearing my agent hat. Generally speaking, this kind of thing should be clear to you as you read, but when in doubt, assume everything applies to both of those people.

Also, as you read this book, you can start at the beginning and work your way to the end (it makes most sense that way). Or you can feel free to skip around and check out the sections that catch your interest first (it works just fine that way, too).

The point is not necessarily the order in which you read, but the relevant information you gather as you read. So relax, knock yourself out, and jump in. Just imagine that you and I are sitting around having coffee and a conversation, talking over the finer points of your last book proposal. (And hopefully you're buying the coffee!)

NOW, BEFORE WE BEGIN…

Of course, there are just a few things you do need to know before we get started.

First, foremost, and always, there is actually only one over-arching reason why any book is published—or rejected:

Profit.

That's it, really.

Remember, publishing is an industry—a business that has at its core the innate desire for survival. And, as for any business, survival means profit. A publishing house that doesn't actively pursue profitability—no matter how noble or sublime its content goals—simply won't be publishing books for very long. Those are just the facts of this capitalist system we've embraced (which also gives us all the opportunity to succeed beyond our wildest dreams!).

So, no matter what book you are currently pitching, you must always keep the idea of profit front and center:

- Remove your "fuzzy focus" lenses.
- Coldly determine what factors influence your publisher's profit potential.
- Position your book's content and market features to highlight profit potential.
- Propagandize your book's proposal to hammer home that profit potential for the publisher. (More on this later.)

THE PUBLISH/REJECT DECISION

Next, you need to be aware of how the "Publish/Reject" decision is made in a publishing board meeting.

Multiple people may weigh in on the decision to publish or reject a manuscript, including the acquisitions editor (your first gatekeeper), an editorial director, a marketing manager or two, a salesperson or two, a print buyer, sometimes a reader or team of readers, and maybe even an employee's nephew or girlfriend or husband or whatever. But in the end, when it's time for the publishing board to decide whether or not to invest in your book, only three voices count: the publisher, the VP of marketing, and the VP of sales.

Oh I know. You're already arguing with me. "What about the acquisitions editor?" you say. "What about the VP of editorial? Certainly those people have a say in the publishing decision, right?"

The honest answer (and I'm sorry to be the one to break it to you…I know this is going to piss off many editorial folks out there): not so much.

You see, the acquisitions editor makes the initial rejection based on what that person thinks his or her publisher, sales VP, and marketing VP will approve later in publishing board. If the acquisitions editor doesn't see your book getting a nod from those three executives, the book gets rejected up front.

If an editor does take your book proposal into that publishing committee meeting, he or she gets no vote on whether it gets published. That's because the primary purpose of any editorial presence at publishing board meetings is simply to be an advocate for whatever book is being presented. The acquisitions editor is only there as a guest, given a three- or four-minute window to advocate your book. (No wonder editors are often such irritable people!) Your editor and/or VP of editorial have to literally *sell* their colleagues on your book.

Sometimes this almost feels like used-car hucksterism, with trinkets or gimmicks to capture everyone's attention. (I once knew of an editorial team that dressed up as pirates to pitch a book to their publishing board!) Your editors have to pitch your book to their customers (publisher, marketing, sales), deftly disarm or deflect any objections, and then ask for the sale—for the company to open its checkbook and buy your book.

And yes, the VP of editorial is usually given a vote, but that vote is also—almost always—simply a lockstep opinion with whatever the publisher (the VP of editorial's boss) has already decided. In fact, in some houses, the publisher and VP of editorial are even the same person, combining that two-person job into one person's responsibilities (and vote).

I've worked in acquisitions for three different publishing houses, and I've sat in many, many publishing board meetings. In all that time I've never seen a publisher and VP of editorial split their votes. If the publisher and VP of editorial happen to disagree on a book, they typically work it out between them until they can present a united front. And if they can't work it out, the publisher *always* overrules the VP of editorial. That's just the way it works. Sorry.

So, if you want to publish a book, you need to convince the publisher, the VP of marketing, and the VP of sales that your book is worth it.

If you can win over those three people, then not much is going to stand in the way of publishing your book. If you win over only two of the three, then your odds drop to about 50/50. The VP of sales will almost always carry more weight in publishing board than the VP of marketing. But he or she will often have to defer to the publisher.

Still, if the sales department says they can't sell your book—no matter how much the marketing department says they will promote it—then most publishers won't take the risk. They'll side with the sales team and send your book packing. I've only seen a publisher override a sales team once in twenty years…so I guess it can happen, but it's terribly rare. (Oh, and by the way, that publisher was right—the book sold four times as many copies as the sales team projected!)

At any rate, your wisest course of action is simply to set up your proposal so that there are no dissenters among those three executives.

Which, of course, is easier said than done.

This book will help you with that, and to that end I've organized it in three sections: Editorial Reasons for Rejection, Marketing Reasons for Rejection, and Sales Reasons for Rejection. If you can eliminate (or at least diminish) the reasons listed in each section, then you are well on your way to publishing success. (IMHBAO.)[2]

ONE LAST WARNING

One last warning before we go further: I will always be honest with you in this book. Sometimes that may make you angry with me. I apologize in advance…but please don't take it personally. I'm just trying to help you by sharing from my experience in publishing.

It's fine with me if you disagree with what I'm saying, if you discover that your experience has been different from mine, or even if you put a giant red X through any page you dislike! But hopefully you'll still find this information helpful—and profitable—for your writing career.

• • •

All right…Are you ready?

Grab a pen (so you can write notes in the margin, or draw the aforementioned giant X), give yourself permission to dog-ear any pages you want to come back to later (hey, it's your book), and…

Let's go!

Mike Nappa

Spring, 2011

---

2 "In My Humble, But Accurate, Opinion."

{ Part One }

Editorial Reasons for Rejection

{ Reason № 1 }

Your Writing Is Crap

All right yes, it's true: Crap writing gets published. Crap writing often hits the *New York Times* bestseller lists. Crap writing sometimes even gets rave reviews.

But that won't work for you. Here's why:

Most often, crap writing is done by (or ghostwritten for) celebrities. You know, the pop singer who decides that because she can opine seductively about a sexual encounter in a three-and-a-half-minute radio single, she's therefore qualified to write a children's book masterpiece about small town America in the 1940s. Or the self-absorbed athlete who decides that because he's a millionaire, people will buy his novel about a football team's rise to glory. Or the teen actress who pens her life story…at the tender age of sixteen. You get the idea.

But if you're reading this book, my guess is you haven't hit number one on the R&B charts, you never even had a tryout with the Dallas Cowboys, and Disney isn't knocking on your door to star you in a new series for preteens.

What that means is, if you send me crap writing, I'm going to reject you. And I'm not even going to feel bad about it. I'll feel like I'm doing humanity a service by keeping your stinky excrement off bookshelves everywhere.

And that's the number one reason why an editor or agent rejects a book. Because your thinking is sloppy, the messaging is vain or irrelevant, the ideas are trite, the thought construction is ignorant, the content is poorly organized, the presentation is clunky, the word choices are abysmal, and…well, let's just say it gives off an unappetizing odor when exposed to the world and leave it at that.

WHAT YOU CAN DO ABOUT IT…
1. Study the craft of writing.

Take time to learn what makes good writing *good* writing. How? Start by reading books you admire—first for the content, and then a second time to dissect the author's techniques. Next pick up a few good books on writing from your local library or bookstore (see the appendix on page 358 for suggestions). If you have the time, take a few writing classes at a local college. Attend author signings and see if you can ask a question or two. Go ahead and take in a writer's conference as well.

But whatever path your studies take, never assume that writing is something that just anyone can do. Do *not* say to yourself, "I've got a book in me!" (huge cliché anyway) and assume that means you are also competent to write a book.

Don't live on the false hope that the fantastic awesomeness of your idea somehow overrides your inexperience and ineptitude with the English language. It won't. Hey, you'd never assume you could pick up a cello and immediately play in the London Symphony, would you? So take the time to study the craft. It'll pay off for you when your book proposal reaches my desk and smells like perfume instead of…well, you know.

2. Nitpick every word.

Some think that writing means putting words on a page. That couldn't be further from the truth. True writing means putting *the right words* on the page—on every page. So, before you send writing samples to me (or to any publishing professional), nitpick every word of every sentence in every paragraph of your work. Try to telescope from the macro (the big picture, plot, message, and progression) to the micro (the individual sentences, words, and paragraph structure) and back again. This means changing your thought perspective and approaching your work from different lines of sight several times. What's your overall, big picture? Once that's defined, zoom in on your plot structure—how does it reinforce the big picture? Then examine your paragraphs—does each and every one add to the plot and the overall big picture, or distract from it? Which individual words enliven the story, which distract? You get the idea. Sure, this kind of detail writing takes time and effort, but you didn't think it'd be easy to publish, did you? Do this until every word justifies its inclusion in your masterpiece, and until everything from the start to the finish demands that the reader keep reading.

My suggestion? Write your manuscript a minimum of three times before anybody else sees it. First, write just to get the words on the paper (or into your computer file). Then rewrite to get the *right words* into the book—ruthlessly deleting the excess, harshly rewording lines that are unclear, trimming and slicing to make a concise, compelling whole. Then rewrite yet again to make sure your "right words" aren't really the wrong words in disguise. After you've put that much time and attention into writing your manuscript three times, you'll likely be remarkably sick of the art you've created. Only then is it ready to show an editor.

3. Never, don't ever, neverneverneverneverevernever send out less than your best.

Look, "good enough" is never good enough. So don't hope that it is and then send it on its way. Instead, strive to shape every manuscript into a work of art that's painted with words. That's the first step toward success in your writing career. And sure, it's a big commitment. Are you willing to take that first step?

You Lied to Me

Dear Mr. Nappa,
I'm pleased to send your publishing company a
guaranteed bestseller...

• • •

Dear Mike,
After studying your company, I'm confident you
will be overjoyed about receiving my proposal for
a new romance series based in 1800s Georgia...

• • •

Dear Nappaland Literary Agency,
Here is the proposal you requested to see...

• • •

What do the authors of all three of these letters have in common? They're all big fat liars. What's worse is they think they won't immediately be seen as liars—they actually think I will swallow their overhyped exaggerations and will fall all over myself to represent their work to publishers.

Wrong.

All these letters do is tell me these writers don't have legitimate talent, so they've turned to exaggeration and half-truth in hopes that they will be acceptable substitutes. Trouble is, this is one of the recurring mistakes beginning writers make—I saw it repeatedly when I was an acquisitions editor, and I continue to see it at my literary agency. It always ends badly. For instance, I once got a query from a writer who crowed, "The market for this book should rival that for the Holy Bible!" He's telling me his book will best the bestselling book of all time? Seriously? He's lying—and we both know it.

But still, desperate writers resort to desperate fictions like these (and many others!) to get agents and/or editors to read their books, blissfully unaware of the self-sabotage they are wreaking.

Take those three sample letters above (all of which are amalgams of real letters I've received). If there really were a way to "guarantee" a bestseller, we'd all be rich already and wouldn't need you. Or even better, you could simply self-publish, make millions, and happily thumb your nose at all rejection-writing jerks like me. Likewise, if you really had studied my company—if you'd paid attention to the categories I focus on, read submission guidelines, and so on—you'd know that there's no way I'm going to represent your romance novel—and that I require a reference from an existing

Nappaland author before I'll even look at your work. And that poor third bloke must think I'm an idiot. If I had actually requested to see your proposal, I'd recognize your name, or at least have your title in my "pending" log. You get the idea.

These tactics of exaggeration or white lying never work. At this point, people on my side of the desk have all heard the most creative truth-stretching efforts hundreds of times. Those little lies may seem new and exciting to you, but they are easier to spot than you think. Still, people send them on, no doubt giggling with mischievous glory as they envision how their little deception has tricked us into reading their subsequent delightful prose. These writers are like a child who claims before-dinner innocence while chocolate chip cookie-smear still paints his cheeks.

Listen, as soon as you lie to me, our relationship is over. I'm not even going to read past your cover letter. Consider your book rejected.

WHAT YOU CAN DO ABOUT IT...

1. Let your writing do the talking.

You know what makes me want to represent a book? The book. Not your cover letter. Not your exaggerated promises. Not your *American-Idol*-wannabe pseudo confidence. Not your faked attempts at professional connection. Not even your purty grin and cowpoke sense o' humor.

So when you're pitching a book, don't look for ways to tell

me what you think I want to hear. Don't try to talk me into reading your book by shading the truth about it or about you. Don't try to impress me with a few little white lies. Chances are, you'll only end up irritating me.

Instead, get me into your writing samples honestly, with realistic expectations and a basic promise that you won't waste my time. That's what matters. Just shut up and let your writing do the talking. If it's got the potential you think it does, you'll hear from me (and others like me).

2. Don't assume you need a gimmick to get my attention.

This is the realm of the immature writer. It's a person who doesn't feel confident about suggestion #1 above. But you must remember, even though it's hard initially to get through to an agent or an editor, we all make money when someone like you does get through with something salable and well-crafted. So there's no need for you to "gimmick" your way in the door with false pretenses or hype or even colorful proposal packages. (Let's face it, if your writing's not good, you're just wasting that confetti you put in the envelope.)

Get out of the gimmick business. Get into the writing business. That's how you'll get my attention.

3. Make honesty your best policy.

Honesty is always the best way to approach a new editor or agent. It may not always get you what you want, but it will usually get you a measure of respect…and respect goes a long way in publishing circles.

For instance, as a rule I don't read new authors without a recommendation from an existing Nappaland author or industry associate (such as an editor I've worked with or a colleague I respect). But I will admit to occasional lapses in this policy. I have, on rare occasions, gotten a query from an author that said something like, "I know you don't normally read 'cold call' submissions, and I certainly respect that. But after studying your agency and examining the kinds of books you've been successful with, I honestly believe you might be interested in my new book. I'd like to ask you to make an exception just this once. May I send you the proposal for…"

This author has been honest with me—and although I don't always make an exception, I do always respect honesty. Because of that, this writer might get a second look.

{ Reason № 3 }

You Insulted Me or My Company

I magine that I come to your house for dinner.

After you've graciously invited me in, I learn that you and your family are headed to Disney World for vacation this summer. Well, of course, I want to go along! So I say to you the following:

"You know, my daughter is lovely! In fact, my daughter is so wonderful that, by comparison, she makes your kids look like rejects from an Ugliest Dog competition. I mean, seriously, look at your oldest child there. Those terribly crooked teeth are just awful! And your middle kid? Wow, is that the North Star on his forehead? Oh no, it's just a Goliath-sized pimple. Gross! And I can see that your new baby obviously takes after her daddy…Well, at least plastic surgery will be an option when she's older, right?"

I smile contentedly at you and your family. "Now," I say, "wouldn't you like my lovely daughter and me to join your family on that Disney vacation?"

Three guesses what kind of response I'm going to get—and

the first two guesses don't count! After insulting your family, chances are very slim that you're going to invite me to join you on the Pirates of the Caribbean ride or to mix with Mickey and Minnie Mouse when your kids go to a Disney character breakfast.

Surprisingly, many authors think nothing of taking that same insulting approach toward an editor or publishing house. For instance, my wife is an executive editor at a midsize publisher, and she came home rolling her eyes recently.

"First," she said, "this writer sent me a pitch with the sappiest, silliest title ever." (It was something like *The Glorious Bride* or *The Marriage Bride* or whatever—and no, it wasn't a book about marriage.) "Then, she belittled the competition," my wife continued, "including two books I published—which we are still selling, and selling well."

Want to guess where that author's proposal ended up? Yep. Rejection-ville.

Do you see why it ended up there?

In the first place, my wife—a well-educated corporate professional—was intellectually insulted by the overly simplistic, sappy title. Honestly, this writer was lucky that my wife looked past the title and dug into the rest of the proposal. (I wouldn't have.)

Next, in an attempt to build up her own book, this writer actually tore down the work of the editor to whom she sent the proposal. Regardless of whether the writer's critiques were valid, you simply don't insult a publisher's current list of books as a means of getting that publisher to add your book to a future list. That just makes no sense.

Other writers insult an editor by speaking disparagingly of authors she's been associated with in the past, by taking a tone of condescension in a cover letter ("Of course you wouldn't know this, but as my book will show, 2 plus 2 actually equals 4!"), by garbling the editor's name, by addressing a "Mr." as "Ms." (or vice versa), or by simply approaching the editor with an overall sense of disrespect.

Most often these insults are unintended, but the result is still the same—another ticket to Rejection-ville.

WHAT YOU CAN DO ABOUT IT...

1. Know your audience.

The lesson here is simple: If you want to increase your chances of publishing success, then take care not to insult the editor or the publishing house—even by accident! The best way to do that is simply to know your audience.

Before you send something to an editor, find out what that editor has worked on in the past, both in her current position and at previous companies. Look through the publisher's website to see what they've done recently in your area—and to gauge whether they've been successful with those books. See if you can discover career highlights for your editor. Look at the editor's blog to see what she values, or which books he admires. Find out what the publisher as a whole seems to be proud of…and then avoid speaking disparagingly of anything on that list.

As with any relationship, the more you know about a person (in this case, the editor), the better you will be at tailoring your interactions with that person—and avoiding inadvertent insults that could sabotage your publishing efforts.

2. Be tactful.

After reading this section, you might be thinking, "OK, I should be sure to avoid comparing my book to anything that the publisher has already released." That's exactly the *wrong* message to take from this section.

There's actually nothing wrong with comparing your book to a book (or books) that the desired publisher has already released. In fact, you *should* be able to show how your proposed work is more than just a rehash of what they've done in the past. *But* you must also be tactful in the way you do that. Try to remember that simply tearing down another product doesn't necessarily lift up your product. It's better to take a "gap" approach to critiquing. That is, identify areas in which the other product is strong but also show the gaps in that strength—and how your product fills those gaps. Ask yourself, "If this were a child, how might I tactfully communicate a critique without insulting or disrespecting the child?" Let your answer guide the way you articulate yourself in your book proposal.

3. Be complimentary.

A little sucking up never hurt any aspiring writer—especially if your flattery is true. If you know the editor was involved in a successful project in the past, go ahead and compliment her on that. You might say something like, "After seeing your fine work on *The Blah Blah Book*, I'm betting that you'll be just the right person to handle my book..."

Also, go ahead and compliment the publishing house as a whole on its recent line of books, or on its reputation with authors, or on its status in the industry. Doing so communicates that you both know this company and are eager to support its success. Plus, it diminishes the number of opportunities you have to lob an unintended insult.

So go ahead and say something nice...it just might pay off.

{ Reason № 4 }

We're Already Publishing a Similar Book

Honestly, this reason for rejection isn't bad for you. It just means you were a little slow getting to market. I've been on both sides of this little equation—as an author and as an editor—and I can tell you this:

Hey, it happens. Get over it.

Not long ago I was pitching a book for one of my authors that was drawn from an academic study he'd done about what families experience at church. It was a great book, solidly based in relevant research, written by a bestselling and award-winning author, and—despite its academic pedigree—was easily readable and relatable. I figured I'd have no trouble selling this book, and so I started pitching it with enthusiasm to editors.

The first editor responded quickly, within a week. They were already planning a book on a similar topic. Rejection number one for our book. A second editor responded just a few days later with the same message. Then a third. Pretty soon it became clear that we were behind the curve on this topic, and despite all our book had going for it, about a half dozen publishers had already gone ahead with plans for different books that addressed the same issues as ours did.

Now, eventually I was able to connect with a few publishers who hadn't yet moved that direction with their publishing list, and in the end, we had two offers to choose from. But for a while there, I have to be honest and say it looked like we might get left out in the cold.

Was it because our proposal was inherently weak or unsaleable? Nope. It was all a matter of timing—and we hadn't timed our proposal right.

That might be your experience as well. You may have a great book with great market potential, but if someone has already beat you to it at a particular publishing house, you'll just have to take your rejection and move on to the next place.

Hey, it happens. Get over it.

WHAT YOU CAN DO ABOUT IT...

1. Consider this kind of rejection good news—and act accordingly.

If one publishing house is already planning a book similar to yours, that means you've correctly identified a publishing trend. Way to go, you!

Sure, you're a little late to capitalize on that trend with this particular publisher, but chances are good another publisher out there hasn't moved as quickly on the trend. So, armed with the knowledge that you are in the forefront of an upcoming movement, you can begin doing deeper market analysis to find a competing publisher to sell on your idea. Who knows, your book might end up outselling the one the first publisher signed ahead of yours.

Ah, poetic justice is sweet, isn't it?

2. Write something new and submit it to the same editor.

If an editor tells you that the reason for rejection is quality, or marketability, or the fact that your momma dresses you funny, well you've already made the wrong impression.

However, if the editor tells you that the only reason she's rejecting your book is because she's already got one like it in the works, that means a) you and this editor think alike, and b) she probably liked your writing—or was at least willing to give your writing a good, hard look.

Hm. An editor thinks like you, and she likes your writing. That sounds like a formula for optimism, despite the current rejection. So determine to take advantage of that.

Get back to your desk. Study the other categories this editor likes to publish in, and then create an all-new proposal that will appeal to that editor's interests. Polish it, and send it off within the next one to three months (long enough so you don't seem desperate, but short enough so she'll still recognize your name). Based on the last rejection, chances are good the editor will give this new book a closer look than a typical one that comes in through the slush pile. That may be all you need to get your foot in the door.

How do I know this? Because it's a tactic that's been used on me more than once. And it worked at least 50 percent of the time.

3. Do some trend forecasting.

If it really is too late to publish the book you've got—if too many publishers are already planning to release a similar book—then maybe it's time to assess the current and upcoming trends in publishing.

Go ahead and take a break from writing and begin searching for data that'll reveal future trends. Check out the last twelve months of bestseller lists. Look for current publishing stats and reports (I like to visit Bowker.com from time to time to see what they've got there). See what's in the planning stages for movie releases and upcoming TV offerings. Look at the online catalogs of your target publishers and check out their "New and Upcoming Releases" tabs.

Bring all this research into your creative mind, and sift through it to see what trends are appearing. Then use that insider info to help you shape and pitch your next book—before someone else beats you to the editor.

{ Reason № 5 }

Your Target Audience Is Too Big

Here's something you must remember: *If you write a book for everyone, no one will buy it.*

I'm serious. Give up your dreams of mass appeal and worldwide acclaim. Every successful book—even ones that achieve mass appeal and worldwide acclaim—started as something for one specific person or one clearly identifiable group of people.

Right now, some of you out there are already shaking your heads at me. "But my book is for everyone," you say. "It has something that all people will enjoy—old, young, man, woman, why even my Chow puppy, Chloe, wags her tail when I read it aloud!"

Let me be the one to tell you that your belief in this area simply isn't true. Yes, of course, some books do end up reaching a broad audience—and good for them. But every one of those books started out with a clearly defined target audience.

Remember *Harry Potter*? Written for kids.

Only after children (and their teachers) started buzzing about the books did their audience expand to parents, then teens, then other adults. But imagine what would have happened if J.K. Rowling had started writing without her target audience (kids) in mind. It's likely she would have soft-pedaled some of the creative slapstick (Bertie Bott's, anyone?) and been more wary of dealing with topics potentially offensive to adults (such as child abuse and bullying).

Remember *The Purpose Driven Life*? Written first for church leaders (as *The Purpose Driven Church*).

After Rick Warren's success with the church leader market, his Christian publisher was happy to expand the content for the average churchgoer in *The Purpose Driven Life*. Only after those church folks started talking about it and sharing the book with their friends, neighbors, and coworkers did it grow to phenomenon status.

Remember that absurd bestselling mash-up, *Pride and Prejudice and Zombies*? Written for college kids with a sense of humor and an appreciation for both horror stories and classic literature. Hard to imagine a more distinct target audience...or to predict the runaway bestseller status this book achieved after college kids started spreading the word to older coworkers and younger siblings.

Do you see where we're going with this? If you want to appeal to the masses, make sure you appeal to the one. If you try to write with everybody in mind, you'll appeal to no one because everyone will think your book is for someone else.

That's why I routinely reject any proposal that tries to tell me the target audience is "the general reader" or "Americans" or "old and young alike" or whatever other term the kids are using these days. I've learned the hard way this simple truth:

If you write a book for everyone, no one will buy it.

WHAT YOU CAN DO ABOUT IT...

1. Identify one representative person who will buy your book.

My friend Mikal is one of the best advertising copywriters and editors I've ever known. Once I walked by his desk and saw a framed picture of some strange woman next to his computer. Now, I've met Mikal's family, and this woman was not part of the clan, so I asked him who she was.

Her name, he told me, was Donna. She was in her mid-thirties. She worked part time outside the home but also spent a lot of time and effort managing her household. She was a mother of three, with some college education. She cared passionately about her family, her faith, and her future.

And—representatively speaking—she was the typical woman who would buy what he was writing.

You probably won't be surprised to discover that Mikal has been very successful in a publishing career that spans advertising, authoring, and editing. Why? Because he knows how to identify and personalize a target audience. Instead of writing for some bland, generic "everyone," Mikal writes for Donna…and all the Donnas (regardless of their actual names) out there respond with their checkbooks.[3]

So you do the same. Find your Donna, know your Donna, and write for your Donna. If you really want to write for everyone, you must first learn to write for one.

2. Don't be lazy.

If it seems a big chore for you to clearly identify one specific target reader and audience, then you aren't working hard enough. You must discipline yourself to think like your reader—and to do that, you must be able to identify and relate to that reader. Sometimes, though, authors think that's too hard, or too time consuming, or too limiting.

These are the authors who typically remain unpublished, or who resort to self-publishing with no real hope of reaching beyond their family and friends with their books.

If your writing is so muddled and unfocused that you can't state immediately and with conviction who your primary audience is, then you haven't done enough work to define your content and your message. That's a formula for failure. So

---

3 On a side note…For his picture of "Donna," Mikal simply cut out a photo of a model from one of the magazines his company publishes. A year or two later, that model actually came to town to visit the publishing house and take a tour. Imagine her surprise—and Mikal's stammering explanation—when she walked by his desk and saw her own face framed and displayed beside his computer!

don't be lazy. Do the hard work it takes to definitely answer the question: *Who* is going to buy this book?

3. Memorize this principle.

"If you write for everyone, no one will buy. If you write for one, everyone who feels like that one will buy."

{ Reason № 6 }

Your Target Audience Is Too Small

Now, if you've just finished reading Reason #5, you may be looking at Reason #6 above and saying to yourself, "Mike, you big hypocrite! You just told me to target 'the one' for my audience, and now you're telling me I need to target a bigger audience. What's up with you, anyway?"

OK, stick with me on this and (hopefully) it'll all make sense.

First, everything I said in Reason #5 is absolutely true. At the same time, when you are identifying the representative "one" who is your target reader, you also have to make sure there are enough of those "ones" to form an affinity group large enough to support the publication of your book. As publishing expert Robert Bly says, "A book aimed at a major publisher must appeal to an audience of hundreds of thousands of people, if not millions. To sell your idea to the editor, you must demonstrate that such an audience exists."[4]

For instance, a target audience of "Marjorie, who is

---

4   Robert Bly, *88 Money-Making Writing Jobs* (Naperville, IL: Sourcebooks, 2009), 41.

pregnant with her first child," is a specific kind of woman in a specific life situation. At the same time, there are hundreds of thousands of newly pregnant women in America during any given year. Voilà! You've just identified a significant, yet specific, target audience: "Women pregnant with their first child." Your target audience is neither too big ("everyone") nor too small.

Ah, but what if your target audience is "Marjorie, who doesn't eat meat, who is pregnant with her first child, and also an avid motocross racer"?

Well, your target is certainly a specific kind of woman in a specific life situation…but there likely aren't very many women who fit that demographic in America. Certainly not enough pregnant vegetarian motocross racers to support the publication of your book. In this instance, your target market is too much of a niche—and that will be cause for rejection.

One hard truth is that a book rejected because of a "niche target audience" is often the kind of book that actually deserves to be published. I remember sitting in a publishing board meeting once, and our children's editor brought a book to the table. "This book won't make any money," she said, "but we should publish it anyway."

It was a picture book for children hospitalized with terminal diseases—a book to help them learn how to die. On a moral/human level, if only one child or one family benefited from that book, it would have been worth it. But, realistically, how many parents would buy this picture book on death instead of *Pat the Bunny* or *If You Give a Mouse a Cookie*? On a practical level, the target audience—though worthwhile—was just too small to justify publishing.

When I left the meeting, I was impressed because the executives had given tentative approval to go ahead and publish this book despite its lack of profit potential. At the time I felt proud to be part of that team. But it is now several years later, and I still haven't seen that book in any catalog. Sad, but true.

And just another reason why even worthwhile books often wind up not getting published.

WHAT YOU CAN DO ABOUT IT...

1. Identify your audience in terms of definable reach.

Yes it's true that you can't write for everyone, but at the same time you must be sure there are enough people who fit your chosen demographic to support the publication of your book. So find your target "one" person, and then see who surrounds him or her in life—and discover what they all have in common.

For instance, if your target "one" is "Bob who likes to collect cars," then you'll want to establish for the editor that there are enough people like Bob out there who'll want to buy your book. For instance, you might identify affinity groups like *Car Collector Magazine* subscribers, or autoworkers, or mechanics and auto body shop workers, or affluent car own-ers, and so on. Then, for your proposal, you would list your target audience with one over-arching identifier: "car enthusi-asts," followed by a parenthetical note that points the editor to the people groups you've tagged.

2. Remove unnecessary limiters.

Yes, you need to know the demographics of your target audience, but some of the things that relate to that audience are things you can keep in your head instead of including in your proposal.

If your proposal really is for vegetarian, pregnant moto-cross enthusiasts—well, first, good luck. But second, you don't necessarily need to point out every single one of those demographic limiters to the editor. Pick the most easily identifiable of the reader traits and highlight that exclusively. In this case, you could probably show a strong target audience of vegetarians and do just fine with that. Or pregnant women as an affinity group. Or probably even motocross enthusiasts.

The point is, pick one of those instead of all three to promote as the primary audience in your proposal. That'll give you more clarity in your writing, and also give the editor a clearer sense of who will want to read your book when it's published.

3. Consider the possibility that your book is about something bigger than you think it is.

When I was working at one publishing house, I got a book manuscript handed to me late in the process. It was already in the catalog and was scheduled to release in only a matter of months. The stated topic and our marketing focus for the book was infertility, so the target audience was "women who have suffered with infertility."

As I started reading the manuscript, I realized that while the author's struggle with infertility was certainly part of the content, the book as a whole was actually a beautiful story about dealing with disappointment—a much broader topic that would appeal to a broader group of adult women. I worried that the narrowly defined target audience we were marketing to wouldn't be enough to support this book—and I felt the book deserved to be read by many more women than simply those who were involuntarily childless.

But it was too late. The book went out and was promptly ignored. We simply couldn't reach enough of our identified niche audience to sell the book in quantity. I still wish someone before me had noticed that this book was about an issue bigger than infertility. If we had, we would have targeted a broader affinity group and found a much deeper pool of potential buyers.

So take the lesson from this, and if your target audience seems too small, reevaluate what your book is really about.

Maybe you too will find that it centers on a theme bigger than your initial thinking. And that could be the difference that gets your book published.

{ Reason № 7 }

Your Target Audience Isn't My Target Audience

If you look at my listing in the *Guide to Literary Agents*, you'll see the following comments: "Does not want to receive children's books, movie or television scripts, textbooks, short stories, stage plays, or poetry."

The reason for including this note in my listing is simple: The people who buy those books are not my audience. I don't have the means or the impetus to try to reach them—so I don't even try.

In spite of that, I recently received an author query for a flip chart of safety tips for children. I also received a proposal for a seven-volume textbook series covering philosophy and history in depth.

Guess who wasted the most time on these proposals?

Not me. I rejected both in less than sixty seconds. These two authors invested lots of time and effort in their writing and in their pitches to me. What they didn't do was pay attention to *my* target audiences—and the result was that they simply wasted their time by trying to contact me with these books.

Now, both these books may be worthwhile and genuinely publishable, and both these authors may be remarkable talents, but from my perspective that doesn't matter. I'll reject these kinds of books every time, simply because they are intended for an audience I don't reach.

By the same token, when I was an editor acquiring suspense fiction, I routinely rejected romance novels and youth fiction and even highbrow literary fiction. Why? They didn't appeal to the audience (thriller readers) I was targeting editorially.

Look at it this way: Let's assume I'm buying lunch for everyone in my neighborhood this Saturday. My neighbors have spoken: They want In-N-Out Burger hamburgers. So I hop a plane to Anaheim, California, to pick up said burgers.

While I'm waiting in line, you appear by my side. "Look!" you say with enthusiasm. "I've got exactly what your neighbors want for lunch." Then you smile, reach into your backpack, and pull out…a Nerf football.

Sounds absurd, doesn't it? There's no way I'm going to serve your Nerf football to my neighbors when I know what they want are In-N-Out Double-Doubles with cheese.

Likewise, editors and agents serve the unique tastes of specific audiences. If my readers want creative ideas for families and you try to sell me a romance novel instead, that's as absurd as trying to sell a Nerf football sandwich to a guy whose mouth is watering for In-N-Out deliciousness. Or if I'm a women's publisher and you pitch me your textbook about prostate cancer, well, don't be surprised when you get my rejection letter.

If you want to avoid my rejection letter, you've got to first make sure that your target audience is the same as my target audience.

WHAT YOU CAN DO ABOUT IT...

1. Visit the "neighborhood" where your target publisher lives.

Of course I don't mean that you should go stand around on the street corner outside the HarperCollins offices in New York City, or that you should begin obsessively stalking an editor. What I mean is that you should become familiar with the audiences your target publishers (or literary agencies) are trying to reach. Who is buying the books this publisher brings to market? What people groups are keeping that literary agency in business?

Spend time on a few websites, checking out recent titles, reading comments from customers, identifying which affinity groups are attracted to which products. If you spend enough time in that "neighborhood," you'll know pretty clearly who the priority target audience is—who the readers are that make up the core of a publisher's business. Then you'll also know how to manipulate my priorities to fit your publishing goals. All you have to do is show me how your book will be over-whelmingly desired by my main target audience.

How would I be able to resist that?

2. Don't assume that you are the exception.

My experience has been that everyone thinks of himself or herself as the exception. "I know you don't normally try to publish for the scuba diver audience, but *my* book is so unique and special, I'm sure you'll want to look at it anyway!"

Yawn.

It's a pretty simple equation. Does your book appeal to my target audience? If yes, then I'll probably give it a look. If no, then I won't. Same goes for just about any other literary agent or publisher. If your book doesn't fit a certain market, don't waste your valuable time sending to editors who never appeal to that market. Don't send kids, books to adult editors. Don't send fiction to nonfiction agents. Don't send a politically conservative book to a company that always publishes books espousing liberal viewpoints.

Put simply, don't assume you're the exception.

3. Avoid mass mailings of your pitch.

Look, there's nothing wrong with sending your pitch out to dozens of agents and/or editors. Sometimes that's what it takes to get the break that you need. But some writers interpret that to mean you should send your pitch out to *any* agent or editor. That's just lazy and stupid—and actually results in more work for you than it should.

Before you send anything, you should first create a list (or a database or whatever) of your targets (agents or editors).

And each target should have an audience affiliation assigned to it. Then, when it's time to pitch your new bestseller, find the editors who target the same audience your book does, and *send your pitch to people who might actually want to buy it.*

Shocking idea, no? But in the end, you are the one who benefits most by sending me books my audience wants to read. So skip the grunt work inherent in a mass-mailing mentality, and instead focus on sending your work to a gatekeeper whose audience matches the one you're trying to reach. Believe me, you'll be glad you did.

{ Reason № 8 }

Your Book Is Too Extreme

OK, I'm not making this up.

One day I was sorting through the mail for Nappaland Literary Agency and I came upon a pitch from some now-nameless author. I opened the envelope and discovered it was a proposal for a book on the topic of abstinence.

Now, I'm all for abstinence as a means of safely managing a person's sex life before marriage, *but*…this guy's "guaranteed plan for celibacy" made me shudder all the way down to my man parts. His great idea?

Castration.

Yep, that was the message of his book. Guaranteed abstinence through voluntary castration. As far as this author was concerned, if guys would just snip a few things off, there'd be no more problems like unwanted teen pregnancies, AIDS, or sexually transmitted diseases.

To which I could only say, "Brrwwrrr!"

I'll tell you the truth, I never even responded to that nutcase.

I simply tossed his little proposal into the recycle bin.[5]

It was almost like a scene from the classic sitcom *Friends*. In one particular episode, one of the main characters, Phoebe (played by Lisa Kudrow), goes out with a guy she met at the coffee shop. During dinner, she invites her date to tell about himself. "I write erotic novels for children," he says with a smile. "They're wildly unpopular." Needless to say, our good Phoebe quickly rejected that would-be suitor, just as I'm sure he'd already been rejected by editors and agents alike.

The point is—as with a book on voluntary castration or pornographic novels for children—sometimes a proposal is rejected by an agent or editor simply because it's too extreme in viewpoint or message.

For instance, if you want to write a book extolling the virtues of Adolf Hitler or Osama Bin Laden, you're going to have a hard time finding a publisher. If you think there should be a book stating that incest is an inalienable right for Americans, or if you want to write a nonfiction treatise explaining why you're certain that the president of the United States is actually a futuristic robot controlled by aliens in the year 2421... Well, you can guess which recycle bin those book proposals will end up filling.

After all, nobody really wants to pay you for a book that demands testicle removal as a lifestyle choice. Got it?

---

5 I found out later that my teenage son thought it was so funny, he rescued the proposal from the trash and scared all his friends with it!

WHAT YOU CAN DO ABOUT IT...

1. Don't assume your nutty ideas deserve to be in print.

Honestly, we all have nutty ideas from time to time. For example, I once thought a book of tear-off, iron-on T-shirt designs was a surefire winner. I look at my notes on that proposal now and I can't believe I actually sent that out to publishers. So, you know, everybody has less than stellar ideas from time to time. (Yes, that book continues to be unpublished.)

Just because you feel passionate about some obscure viewpoint doesn't mean you should pursue publication of that idea—especially if you are still trying to build your reputation as a writer. Just put that extreme idea in a file cabinet somewhere and move on to something that's more likely to have success.

And hey, look at the bright side. If you ever do hit the big time as an author, you can use your newfound status (and money) to publish all the extremist literature you want. But for now? Just let it go, friend, let it go.

2. Try fiction.

If you feel strongly about publishing an idea that is just obviously too extreme for most people, try couching that idea in a fictional story. Sometimes that approach can even deliver more impact and literary strength than nonfiction (for instance, George Orwell's *Animal Farm* or William

Golding's *Lord of the Flies*). Plus, it gives you the freedom to manipulate the circumstances of the story to fit your desired outcome and make your extreme ideas seem both normal and progressive.

Sure, fiction like this is mostly propaganda (*Avatar*, anyone?), but it can also reach a broad audience and give you a creative outlet to experiment with your ideas. So, you know, if you must write extremism, fiction could be a good place to start.

3. Try writing from a more balanced perspective.

Honestly, Americans tend to be an open-minded bunch. We'll consider just about any wacky viewpoint as long as it isn't presented as an exclusive, all-or-nothing perspective. So consider publishing a book that explores multiple viewpoints on your given topic—and include your pet perspective with appropriate force and thought as one of the possible options.

For instance, if Mister Castration Guy above were to publish a book called *Four Views on Abstinence*, he might actually have a chance of seeing that in print. Then, as long as he dealt fairly with other views, he could easily include his extremist view as one option in the book. Most people wouldn't object to that.

What's more, if you are open-minded enough to talk about other viewpoints in the context of your extremist view, you may actually grow as a person. It may not change your perspective, but at least it will give you insight into other people's perspectives—and increase your publishing potential at the same time.

{ Reason № 9 }

Your Ideas Conflict with My Values and/or My Company's Values

It's a free country, right? Freedom of speech and the press is guaranteed in the First Amendment to the U.S. Constitution. Thus, I can publish anything I want about any topic I want, right?

Well, sort of.

Yes, if you can afford to self-publish, you can say just about anything in print as long as it's not criminal.

Ah, but if you are looking to disseminate your thoughts widely through a formal publishing house, in book form, well, your freedom of speech just got a lot less free.

It's kind of the obvious, dirty little secret in publishing, but those in power tend to stifle viewpoints that don't match their values. This applies to the values of an overall corporation as much as it does to an individual editor's values.

Or, to put it another way: yes, I will censor you by not publishing you.

And if enough of us choose to do that, you will effectively be silenced by our society.

On the one hand, this type of censorship is a necessary byproduct of capitalism. We publish what our audiences will buy. Our audiences tend to adhere to certain value sets, so we do too. Additionally, my right to freedom of speech includes with it a guarantee that I can't legally be forced to print viewpoints I find disagreeable or not in keeping with my values. Those are good things, with self-correcting social mechanisms that actually work in our favor…

…Unless you are on the wrong side of the values continuum and find yourself shut off from the privileges of publishing.

And make no mistake, this happens over trivial values as much as it does over the "biggies" in the moral universe. I've seen books rejected by some publishers for being "too religious" that were then rejected by others for being "not religious enough." I've seen books rejected because an editor disliked the author's political views, or because an editor was offended by violence or because a story wasn't violent enough or because a politically incorrect word was used or because an editor hated cats or because an editor was an avid environmentalist or because an editor was *not* an environmentalist or…well, you name just about anything a person can have an opinion about, and that's been a reason for rejection.

At any rate, we can't ignore that an editorial rejection of a manuscript is, at its purest, a human decision. Every human decision is governed by the values ingrained in the person making that decision.

Thus, if you send me a book proposal that grates against my values (say, a book promoting voluntary castration or a story that features cats as anything besides spawn of Satan), I'm going to reject it.

As they say in politics, values matter.

WHAT YOU CAN DO ABOUT IT...

1. Find out who in publishing shares your values.

For starters, while not all viewpoints are welcome at all publishing companies, most viewpoints are certainly welcome at some publishing company somewhere. Because of the broad diversity of opinion in America—and the entrepreneurial spirit inherent in our society—somebody out there probably publishes from a similar value perspective as you. Your job is to find that publisher.

According to Parapublishing.com, there are about four hundred medium- to large-size book publishers in the United States, and thousands more small publishers to boot.[6] So take some time to explore who publishes what, and locate those that appear to share your values. The reference book *Writer's Market* has all kinds of subject indexes that organize publishers according to the types of books they release, and this can help you determine a company's values. Also, you can check corporate websites for mission statements and backlist titles

---

6 "Publishers, Number Of," Parapublishing.com.

that will help you determine whether your values would fit with specific publishing houses.

Once you know who shares your values out there, you'll do a better job of avoiding the ones who don't—and that'll increase your chances of publication as a result.

2. Get to know what your editors value.

Individual editors have their own quirks and values as well, and sometimes that value set will override even the editor's stated corporate values when making a decision about your book. So try to discover what hot buttons elicit reactions, if you can. Often, you can simply ask an editor what his or her passions in publishing are, and that editor will let you know what's important.

Additionally, many editors today blog as part of their job responsibilities. If that's the case with an editor you want to work with, then subscribe to that editor's blog. That person's values will soon come out in the random conversations he or she posts there. And also go ahead and get on an e-newsletter list or two from companies that appeal to you. Those emails will mostly be marketing copy, but they'll also tell you what people inside the building see as valuable and important in their business.

3. Self-publish.

This is, of course, the only true way to express your freedom to speak your mind in print. However, this also discriminates against those who don't have the money to afford it and against those who don't have the knowledge and resources to widely promote a book. Still, no society is perfect, and at least this option exists for you. In many other non-democratic nations, self-publishing material that expresses values against the accepted norms is illegal, so count your blessings where they may be found.

If you find yourself truly locked out of the public conversation because your values or viewpoints are being censored by the decision-makers at America's publishing centers, then self-publishing may be your best option. After all, it's a free country.

{ Reason № 10 }

Your Book Tries to Do Too Much

This is another mistake that most beginning authors make—trying to cram too much into one book. It's a problem that shows up most often in nonfiction books, but you fiction writers out there should also beware.

If you're trying to combine two or more distinct subtopics, or two or more significant storylines, they'd better have a clear convergence and obvious relevance with each other. Otherwise, people who like one subtopic or story will be annoyed by the disruption caused by the other—and many will actually give up before they get to the end simply because they're tired of the interference.

This is the rule: "One book, one message." If you break that rule, be prepared for the heartbreak of a rejection.

A good writer is also a patient writer. You don't have to hit every important topic or storyline in every book; you only need to talk about the relevant ones. Those other important topics can wait until they can be dealt with in depth in a book of their own.

Orson Scott Card is an excellent example of a writer who understands this principle. In 1983 he'd landed a contract with Tor Books to publish his first full-length science fiction novel—a book called *Speaker for the Dead*, which starred a character from one of his short stories, Ender Wiggin.

"In order to make the Ender Wiggin of *Speaker* make any sense," Card says, "I had to have this really long, kind of boring opening chapter that brought him from the end of the Bugger War to the beginning of the story in *Speaker*." That just wasn't good enough for Card, so he came up with a different option. "The only solution I could think of…was to write a novel version of [my short story] *Ender's Game*, so I could put all that material about how Ender became a Speaker for the Dead at the end of that book, thus allowing *Speaker* to begin at its true beginning."[7]

The result? Decades later, that secondary, "setup" book, *Ender's Game*, is one of the most successful science fiction novels of all time.

Get the point?

WHAT YOU CAN DO ABOUT IT…
1. Memorize this principle: "One book, one message."

I'm a firm believer in the "one book, one message" structure for a manuscript. Meaning, no matter where you look in a

---

7 Orson Scott Card, "Introduction," *Speaker for the Dead: Author's Definitive Edition* (New York: Tor, 1986, 1991), xii–xiii.

book—from chapter one to chapter ninety-nine—the reader should always be able to see how it relates to, and reinforces, the central message of the book as a whole.

So when you're writing, re-think the way you approach each chapter of your book. In the context of your chosen overall message, is this current chapter an intrusion? Or an interesting diversion akin to a rabbit trail? Or is it absolutely necessary to complete the delivery of your message? If it's one of the first two options here, cut it out. Only allow it to stay in your manuscript if it's absolutely necessary to the book as a whole.

If you're brutally critical with yourself on this issue, it saves me from having to be that way…and will likely improve your chances of avoiding my rejection.

2. Be willing to write two (or more) books.

If you're writing a manuscript and you find yourself drawn toward a deeper exploration of a subtopic or side plot, it should set off a red flag in your critical evaluation of your own work. Go ahead and write out your thoughts while they are fresh. Then cut those sections and paste them into a separate computer file where you can look at them independently.

Can you see that subtopic or side plot standing alone? With a little expansion and/or a little more depth, could that material be a book all by itself? I think that 90 percent of the time, if you are honest, your answer will be "yes" to those questions.

Rejoice! That's job security for you. As long as you've got new ideas to write about, you've got new opportunities to publish.

So be smart with your content. Be patient. And like Orson Scott Card, be willing to let your creative energies split into two (or more) different books. Who knows? Your result could be the defining work of a generation.

3. Remember, by writing a book you make a promise to the reader…and you'd better keep it.

Look at the title of this book: *77 Reasons Why Your Book Was Rejected (and how to be sure it won't happen again!)*. Right up front, I've made a promise to you that if you look inside here, you'll find help to avoid rejection in your book publishing career.

What if I wasted your time with an entire section on screenplay writing? Or if I'd opened this book with a broad overview of the history of book publishing in America, you know, as "background" for what was to come later in the book.

Yawn.

You bought this book because you wanted what I promised: *seventy-seven reasons why your book was rejected*. If I don't keep that promise—if I let my tangential interests or inability to maintain focus distract me—then you have every right to reject my book. And if you don't keep your promise because you're trying to do too much in the book proposal you send me…well, you can bet that I'll reject yours.

{ Reason № 11 }

Your Word Count Is Too Long or Too Short

As the story goes, that whole *Twilight* phenomenon Stephenie Meyer started was actually just a publishing mistake made by an inexperienced slush pile assistant.

It seems that in 2003 Ms. Meyer sent a query letter to Writers House agency describing a young adult novel about teen vampires, and asking if they'd be willing to take a look at her 130,000-word manuscript. What neither Ms. Meyer nor this agency underling knew was that young adult fiction is supposed to fall in the 40,000–60,000 word count range. Had a more experienced slush pile gopher received that query, it would have been greeted with a standard form-letter rejection.

Instead, this assistant asked to see the manuscript, liked it, and passed it on to Jodi Reamer at Writers House. Ms. Reamer also liked it despite the bloated word count. She sold it to Little, Brown, and thus began what has since been called "the biggest publishing franchise since *Harry Potter*."[8]

---

8 Katherine Rosman, "The Death of the Slush Pile," *The Wall Street Journal* (January 15, 2010).

Now, if you think that you too will have the same kind of one-in-a-million, extraordinary good luck that Stephenie Meyer had, then by all means skip this section and move blissfully on to the next chapter.

However, if your life tends to be less magical and more like the rest of us, then pay attention, because this reason for rejection is one you can easily escape.

Stephenie Meyer notwithstanding, most of us routinely reject books simply because they don't fit a standard word count. Why? Well, this will sound familiar to you: profit.

It works like this: Just about every book published conforms to a standard trim size—that is, the width, height, and page count of a particular book. That trim size is filled by groupings of pages called "signatures," usually sixteen pages per signature. So, for instance, a 160-page book would hold ten signatures. Publishers know very clearly how many words fit into a sixteen-page signature, and thus try to fit their word counts into signatures that maximize the printing process.

That means extra signatures cost extra money to print. Conversely, smaller signatures mean a lower retail price (simply because we buyers have been conditioned to assume that a thinner book is inherently worth less than a thicker one). Both of those situations have a direct impact on publisher profitability, so they've standardized much of this formula to be sure they can consistently print books that'll make money.

Are there exceptions to this practice? Sure—but they are just that: exceptions.

Now, some writers may assume that if their word count is a bit long or short, editors can just cut where needed or give direction on where to add text. Sure, that could happen. But again, you're asking to be the exception—and assuming an editor will do your job for you when you should instead be doing the editor's job for her (see Reason #31 for more on this). Why take that unnecessary risk?

If you really want to avoid rejection, and actually want to remove an obvious obstacle in the way your book is viewed by an agent or a publishing house, then do the simple thing here.

Write a book that conforms to the word count agents and editors expect.

Or, you know, pray that your query letter is picked up by a newbie on her first day.

Your call.

WHAT YOU CAN DO ABOUT IT...

1. Educate yourself on standard word counts.

Last month I got a note from an editor telling me she was looking for well-crafted historical fiction that ran between 80,000 and 100,000 words. I didn't have anything to show her, so I decided to skulk through the offerings at

Authonomy.com.[9] With patience I found one that looked interesting…but it was only 30,000 words. Rejected.

Later I found another: 145,000 words. Rejected. Believe it or not, I looked at a half dozen historical novels that seemed interesting story-wise—and not a single one of them fell in that 80,000–100,000 word count. I gave up looking.

If any of those authors had taken the time to educate themselves on typical word counts for historical fiction, they might have had a contract by now. So be sure you do find out that info. Some editors will tell you if you simply send an email and ask. You can also look at books similar to yours and get a quick word count estimate by counting all the words on one page and multiplying by the full page count. (That's not exactly accurate, but for your purposes it'll be close enough.)

And, by the way, here are some basic word counts I use when evaluating an author's proposal:

Typical adult nonfiction book: 45,000–55,000 words

Typical adult novel: 80,000–100,000 words

Typical young adult novel: 40,000–60,000 words

Typical juvenile book (fiction or nonfiction): 20,000–40,000 words

Typical children's picture book: 400–600 words (or no words at all!)

---

9 For those who don't know, Authonomy.com is a "writing community site for writers, readers, and publishers, conceived and developed by book editors at HarperCollins."

2. Write toward your target word count.

For nonfiction books this is easy. Simply take your desired word count, subtract the number of words in your front pages and introduction, and then divide the remaining figure by the number of chapters in your book. For instance, if yours is a 50,000-word book with 12 chapters and 2,500 words in front matter/intro, then your equation series would look like this:

$$50,000 - 2,500 = 47,500; 47,500/12 = 3,958$$

That means you'll probably want to shoot for around 4,000 words per chapter. Easy.

For fiction, this is harder because a novelist has to follow the story wherever it goes. So you'll just have to keep benchmarking yourself. If yours is an adult novel, for instance, and you hit the midpoint of your plot at only 28,000 words, you'll need to beef it up a bit. But if you hit 40,000 words and you're still really only at the beginning of your story, then you'll want to start figuring out how to cut back so as to avoid the "abrupt ending" syndrome.

3. Write a different book, or two books.

Got a great novel that reaches a dramatic, satisfying conclusion at 49,000 words? For an adult novel, that's a problem. But for a young adult novel, it'd be right in the target. So, instead of trying to double the size of your word count, why not go back through and edit so it has inherent appeal for teens and college students? Then you can pitch it as a young adult novel and (hopefully) make millions like Stephenie Meyer.

Or, by the same token, if your wide-ranging fantasy novel tops out at 161,000 words, try breaking that book into two books in a series instead. Add a third book and you've got yourself a bona fide trilogy that'll (hopefully) triple your success as an author.

{ Reason № 12 }

You Are Not Credible on the Topic You Want to Write About

I remember once I was pitching a book to publishers that dealt with practical theology and American life in the twenty-first century. I had outlined it all and written the first fifty pages or so, and I sent it out. Not long after, one publisher called me about the book.

"This is very well written," she said. "It has both depth and readability. But you aren't qualified to write it."

I was dumbfounded. "How can you tell me I'm not qualified to write what I've already written?" I asked.

She just shrugged. "You're not a pastor or a seminary professor. There's no way we can sell a book like this unless it was written by someone with those kinds of credentials."

Well, I did find another publisher for that book. And I did write the whole thing—despite my lack of credentials. And it was lauded by critics and reviewers and even won a prestigious national award. But (and I have to grit my teeth to say this), in the end that tactless editor was right. The book sold poorly in the marketplace and never even earned back its advance.

Despite the actual content of my book, the glowing endorsements, and even the award-winning status it earned, the fact that I was neither a pastor nor a seminary professor was enough to limit this book in the eyes of many potential buyers. As far as they were concerned, I wasn't credible on the topic (practical theology) about which I wanted to write.

Working as an agent today, I make the same kinds of judgments about your books that The Tactless One made about mine. If you send me a book on principles of parenting, but you have no children of your own, I'm skeptical. If you think you've got the next great political plan for America, but you've never run for office or held a job in government, chances are good I'll reject. If you want me to represent your book on how to make millions as an entrepreneur, but you're still living in your mother's basement and working part-time at the local coffeehouse, well, something about that situation tells me you might not be credible.

Credibility counts in the marketplace, and that means it's important on the editor's desk as well. If you're not truly a credible authority on your subject of choice, you're going to get a rejection letter. And you just might deserve it.

WHAT YOU CAN DO ABOUT IT...

1. Demonstrate clearly why you can be trusted on the topic.

It's OK if you're not everything everyone would expect as the author of a book on a particular topic. For instance, a man writing a book about the emotional stages of pregnancy might seem wrong at first glance—until you discover that this male author is also an obstetrician with a doctorate in psychology on the side.

A stay-at-home mom may seem unlikely as an author of a book on best practices for business—until she shows that running her household successfully mirrors the management practices of the world's most successful corporations.

The point is, whatever your experiences and credentials are, make sure you clearly show an editor how those things make *you* uniquely qualified to write the book on your chosen topic.

2. Earn the right to speak.

Look, if you want to publish a book about cycling, don't just watch the Tour de France on TV and then assume you've got what it takes. Get out there and get on a bike. Enter a race or two. Train for a championship. Take a few nasty spills on the pavement. Test new equipment. Take apart, and put back together again, your old bicycle. Do whatever it takes to earn the right to speak about cycling, both as an intellectual expert and a physical participant in the sport. Once you've done that, you'll have earned the credibility to write about it.

The same principle applies to just about any topic, and to both nonfiction and fiction. Don't ever let yourself be a writer who is on the outside looking in. Instead, take the time and invest the energy in doing what it takes to earn the right to speak on your particular area of interest. Then you'll not only be credible as a writer…you just might be interesting!

3. Recruit a credible coauthor.

This is the advice that The Tactless Editor gave to me. She actually wanted to publish my book, but she couldn't do it unless I had more credibility on the topic. From her perspective, that was as simple as finding a seminary professor who was willing to loan me his name and credentials as "coauthor" on the book. I, obviously, declined. But, even though I still dislike this idea in general, I can see that it would work both in a publishing board meeting and in the marketplace.

So, if you just don't have the right credentials but you still feel like you can write a great book on the topic, this is an option. Find an established expert on your topic and offer to share both a byline and royalties if he or she will collaborate with you on the book. Who knows? It might be the beginning of a beautiful (and profitable) friendship.

{ Reason № 13 }

You Didn't Do Your Homework

I'm looking at a query letter right now that makes me laugh out loud.

For starters, it's addressed to "Dear Reader." Then it goes on to pitch a four-part series of novels that the author claims will be "as eye-popping as *Baywatch*!" (Yes, the author included that silly exclamation point after "*Baywatch*.") This series, the author promises, will be replete with "violent characters, sexual escapades, drugs, dirty money, foul play, and foul language."

Oh joy.

If this author had done a little homework—say, visiting my agency website for example—that person would have figured out pretty quickly it was a waste of time to send me a "Dear Reader" query for this silly proposal. This is obviously not the kind of book Nappaland Literary represents, making it an easy rejection for me.

Still, even worse than authors who don't do their homework about potential publishing partners are authors who don't do their homework when it comes to content research. This drives me nuts in a manuscript. The author is steaming along, and then all of a sudden he or she reverts to generic references instead of specific ones, or appears to try to fake through a section by glossing over details that would normally be expected.

Look, there's a difference in impact between saying, "She took sleeping pills" and "She took two Ambien, hoping her body hadn't yet built up a tolerance to them." There's a difference between saying, "He was a professional con man" and "With more than a decade of practice, he'd perfected The Pigeon Drop to the point where it was almost a work of art."

The point is this: Do your homework, dummy.

For instance, if you're writing a book about police officers breaking down a crime scene, don't just quote what you've seen on TV. Find out what it took to get a warrant, what kind of evidence collection kits are used for different crimes, what kind of health concerns are associated with the handling of a corpse, what kind of photography is necessary, what fibers and liquids are sought after and collected, and so on.

You've got to make me believe two things: a) I'm the agent (or editor) you're looking for, and b) you're the writer I'm looking for.

Do your homework before you submit your query, and maybe you'll do just that.

WHAT YOU CAN DO ABOUT IT...

1. Never send a "cold call" query.

We'll dig more into this in Reason #14 (following), but for now just live by this rule: "If I don't know you, I won't query you."

Obviously, I'm not suggesting that you try to form personal relationships with every editor or agent to whom you send a query. But I am insisting that you'd better know how to spell my name before you send me a book. And you definitely should know something about my history and the kinds of books I'm looking to publish. You should know a little bit about the history of my publishing house or my agency, and even what books I've done in the past that are similar to the one you want to publish.

Don't know that info? Then don't send me your query. Take the time to do your homework about the market first.

2. Never stop learning.

It's funny to me how many people love the idea of being an author and hate the idea of doing the work of an author. This kind of person thinks that being a writer means simply sitting in front of a computer and letting golden words of wisdom flow straight from the brain into the keyboard. Truth is, actual writing often takes less time than the research needed to put together a winning book.

Listen to this, because it's important: Your content and market research are just as important—and should probably take as much time—as the words you finally put down on paper.

A good rule of thumb is a 1:1 ratio—that is, for every hour of writing time, you should probably spend another hour in content and organizational research. Early in the formation of your book, that ratio will probably look more like 3:1 in favor of research, but as you begin to get deeper into your manuscript it'll start to even out. Then, before you ever send out your book, you'll be wise if you spend an additional twenty to forty hours simply on market research—finding out who publishes what and why, and how that fits into your own hopes for your book.

In short, never stop learning, because the near-constant accumulation of knowledge is what will set you apart.

3. Don't assume the reader won't notice your shortcuts.

One of my authors recently was writing a mystery novel, when all of a sudden she stopped completely. I asked her about it, and she told me simply, "I'm learning how to clean a .22 short mini revolver."

Turns out her book included an organized crime element, and there were a few scenes where guns came into play. Instead of shortcutting the reader with something like, "He pulled a gun and threatened everybody," she insisted on knowing what kind of guns her characters might carry— and also knowing what her characters would know about those guns.

That kind of research added extra hours of work for maybe four or five sentences in her book. But that stubborn refusal to take a shortcut in gun description also made for a more realistic, credible novel.[10]

Adopting that kind of "no shortcuts" attitude will set your story apart as well.

---

10 By the way, just this month we found out that the novel in question had won a national fiction award—so apparently this author's dedication is paying off.

{ Reason № 14 }

You Are Lazy

Want to hear about the stupid, lazy things I did today?

For starters, I planned to spend my morning pitching a couple of my clients' books to publishers and then to dedicate my afternoon to writing more of this book you're reading. A reasonable plan. But I got behind on my morning schedule and started taking shortcuts to speed things up.

First, I whipped off an email query to an editor at Peachtree Publishing. It's a query I'd carefully crafted and even used before, so I barely glanced at it before I sent it. The only problem was…*I'd used it before.*

Apparently I was smart enough to change the salutation at the top of the email, but in the body of the letter I made this bold statement: "I feel confident that you and your team will see this one as a perfect fit in a future line of books from *Workman* Publishing."

I can hear the Peachtree editor grumbling already, "Mike, if this is perfect for Workman, then why'd you send it to *me*?" Grr.

Oh, and it doesn't stop there.

After sending out this inappropriately targeted query, I went back and took a look at my personal notes regarding this editor. (I was hoping we'd connected in the past—and that she might've liked me enough to overlook my faux pas.) Here's what I found: "Do *not* email queries—this editor will not review any submission received this way. All queries and manuscripts must be sent by U.S. Mail."

Double grr. My book is now dead in the eyes of this editor. If I'm lucky, she'll overlook my stupidity and send me a rejection letter. More likely, she'll simply ignore me (something I call the dreaded "pocket rejection") and move on to agents who aren't quite as stupid or lazy as I was today.

As if that wasn't enough, today I also was pitching a new fiction novel for kids to publishers. In my haste to get through my list, I sent a passionate query to an editor at Hyperion.

She rejected the book about four minutes later.

Do you see why? (If not, you're as bad as I am.)

Look at it. I sent the query to *Hyperion* (the adult division) instead of *Hyperion Books for Children* (the kids' book division). Yes, I've got these editors and imprints listed separately in my database. Yes, I should have known better. I was just too lazy to look twice and make sure I got the right info when I copied it out.

So, in the space of about half an hour today, I got two near-instant rejections—and I deserved them both. Why? Because I was lazy.

Lesson learned (again).

And it's one you'd better learn quickly if you want to avoid the same fate as mine today.

WHAT YOU CAN DO ABOUT IT...

1. Measure twice, cut once.

We touched on this a little bit in Reason #13, and now you can see that sometimes it's laziness in the simple things that sabotages our best efforts in the pursuit of publication.

Look, we all know that things like sending out query letters and creating a detailed market analysis are boring and tedious jobs. But attention to detail in those areas can be the difference in whether your book gets read by an agent or an editor.

There's an old proverb among construction workers that goes something like this: "Measure twice, cut once. Measure once, cut twice." The idea here is that if you measure your piece of lumber twice—double-checking to make sure the measurement is accurate—then you avoid making a mistake that could cause you to have to start all over again from scratch.

That's the kind of attitude you must take when sending out queries. Double-check names. Double-check addresses. Make sure you're aiming at the right targets. Do all the mundane detail work that guarantees you get the best result—every time.

2. Treat every editor (or agent) as if he or she is the only one to whom you're sending your book.

Obviously I failed in this area today—and it ruined two opportunities to publish for my authors. You know how rare a publishing opportunity is, so you can guess what an enormous cost my laziness had. Don't make the same mistakes I did.

Yes, when creating a proposal pitch and/or a query letter, you will out of necessity put together a "one size fits all" approach. And you will clearly need to send it out to as many editors and/or agents as you can, because that simply increases your odds of publication. But when I receive your query or pitch, I should *never* be made aware that I am just one of many you are trying to woo. That'd be like asking a whole sorority out for a date. Sure, it's possible that one of the girls in the sorority might be willing to join you for a dance…but not if she thinks you might dump her at any instant if one of the other sisters shows up.

So, tailor your generic pitches with individual editors or agents in mind. Make each of us think we're your number-one choice, and maybe we'll be flattered enough to return the favor.

3. Do what's required to give your book the best opportunity.

Several years ago, an editor friend of mine—let's call her Kelly—spoke at a writer's conference. She met an aspiring author with a great idea for a book. Kelly wanted to publish the book, but it needed just a little bit of extra work to make it something that would pass the publishing committee. So Kelly told this writer exactly what to do to get her book published. "Then send it to me directly," Kelly said, "and I'll take it from there."

Months passed. Nothing.

The next year at the same writer's conference, Kelly saw the author again. "I know I have to get that revised proposal to you," the author said with embarrassment. "I'll do it soon."

Long story short, three years later that author still hasn't done the work Kelly asked for. Yet the author keeps coming back to the writer's conference, trying in vain to find an editor who wants to publish her books.

"I could have published that book," Kelly says now. "In fact, I *would* have published it. But this author was too lazy to follow up."

If you want to publish, you've got to be willing to *do the work* it takes to optimize every opportunity. If you don't want to do the work, all the writer's conferences and workshops in the world won't do you any good. Remember, there's no such thing as a lazy writer…there's only those who get published and those who don't.

{ Reason № 15 }

You Didn't Pass the "First Line Test"

My grandfather, the knife fighter, killed two Germans before he was eighteen."[11]

When I read this first line from David Benioff's book *City of Thieves*, I was hooked. I was actually standing in the grocery store, just passing a few minutes while I waited for my wife. But after that first line, I couldn't bear to part with the book. I ended up buying it along with a gallon of milk and some frozen pizza.

That's the power of a good first line—it demands the reader's attention. It captures the imagination in such a way that the reader can't help but keep going. Consider these classic first lines from literary history:[12]

- "It was a pleasure to burn."—Ray Bradbury in *Fahrenheit 451*

---

11 David Benioff, *City of Thieves* (New York: Plume, 2008, 2009), 1.

12 Hans Bauer, compiler, *In the Beginning: Great First Lines from Your Favorite Books* (San Francisco, CA: Chronicle Books, 1991), 4, 183, 48, 27.

- "Here is Edward Bear, coming downstairs now, bump, bump, bump, on the back of his head, behind Christopher Robin."—A.A. Milne in *Winnie-the-Pooh*
- "If you really want to hear about it, the first thing you'll probably want to know is where I was born, and what my lousy childhood was like, and how my parents were occupied and all before they had me, and all that David Copperfield kind of crap, but I don't feel like going into it, if you want to know the truth."—J.D. Salinger in *The Catcher in the Rye*
- "I met Jack Kennedy in November, 1946."—Norman Mailer in *An American Dream*

What all of these first lines have in common is that they cannot be ignored. Every single one makes you, the reader, ask the question, "Well, what happens next?" And that means it passes the "First Line Test" that so many editors and agents use (myself included).

And you, dear reader? If you can master the art of the first line, well, I'm going to have a hard time rejecting your work. I'll be too busy reading on to find out what happens next.

WHAT YOU CAN DO ABOUT IT...
1. Understand what a first line must accomplish.
The first line of any book—fiction or nonfiction—makes a promise to the reader about the rest of your book. Thus, your first line must accomplish these things:

- *Create curiosity.* It must make the reader ask, "What happens next?"
- *Demonstrate credibility.* It must make the reader believe, "This author can be trusted with my reading time."
- *Evoke emotion.* It must make the reader *feel* something—anticipation, fear, joy, whatever your book needs the reader to feel.

If you can create a first line (and first paragraph) that does these three things, you are already well ahead of your competition—and past the first line of defense from editors and agents who want to reject your work.

2. Read a row of first lines.

This is a simple study exercise that's also fun and effective. If you feel the need to get better at first lines, then inundate yourself with them.

Go to your local bookstore or library and find the section that represents your chosen category of writing. For instance, if you are a business writer, go to the business section, or if you're a crime novelist then go to crime novels section.

Pick a shelf of books in that section, then begin at one end and pull a book off the rack. Open to the introduction or first chapter, read only the first line (or maybe the first paragraph), and then rate that book on a scale of one to ten for its first-line effectiveness. Go all the way down the shelf, rating the first lines of the books you see. Afterward, go back to the books you rated eight or higher and re-read those lines, asking yourself two questions: What is it about this first line that earns a high rating? And what can I learn from that to apply to my own writing?

When you're done, you'll know more about writing than most authors—and you'll be well on your way to crafting a first line that leads to publication.

3. Always ask yourself: will they read on?

I spoke at a writer's conference once and sat in the audience during a panel called, "Will They Read On?" Conference attendees had submitted the first page of any of their works—fiction or nonfiction. One by one, each "first page" was read aloud. Then the panel of agents and editors answered one simple question: "If you had received this proposal, would you read on?"

I was astounded at how many times the answer to that question was "no." That's not because I thought the agents and editors were too tough; rather, it was shocking to hear out loud the number of aspiring writers who had absolutely no idea how to start a book. The two or three that had mastered the craft of the beginning easily stood out.

So use that knowledge to your advantage. Every time you write a first line, or a first paragraph, or a first page, imagine yourself at this writer's conference with people reading aloud your work. And ask yourself, "Will these editors and agents want to read on?"

Keep revising until your answer is irresistibly, unequivocally, *yes*.

{ Reason № 16 }

My Publishing List Is Packed for the Next Eighteen Months

If you have to get rejected (and everyone does at some point), then at least this is a good reason for it. Here's the way it works:

Although there are obvious exceptions (such as the instant biography that appears when just about any celebrity dies), most editors plan their seasonal lists twelve to eighteen months in advance. For instance, this book you're holding in your hands was actually contracted about fourteen months before its initial release. I've had books released as early as nine months after contract, and others released as far off as twenty months. But typically anywhere from twelve to eighteen months is normal.

Additionally, due to resource constraints (including human resources as well as cash flow) and market timing issues, a publishing house can only release a certain number of books in each season. This can be as few as one or two (for small publishers) or as many as a few hundred (for the major New York houses). Regardless, there are still a finite number of slots available in a publishing list each season. Each time a book is approved and contracted, it fills one of those slots.

Now, if I'm planning my spring/summer list for next year and I've only got twenty slots to fill, what am I going to do with that twenty-first book that's contracted? Well, I'll go ahead and drop it into one of the slots for the fall/winter list. But what happens if there are cutbacks at my publishing house and my fall/winter list get trimmed down to only twelve slots? Or what if a series I acquired two years ago is scheduled to release a new book in fall? Or what if last month I got three outstanding proposals that I also contracted and dropped into my fall/winter list?

Well, now it's possible that I'm getting too far ahead in my acquisitions schedule. Instead of being eighteen months out, I may be forced into planning twenty-four or thirty months into the future. That's just too long to be able to predict with any real accuracy the success of a book. Our world moves too fast, and public opinions change too quickly. If I'm smart (and most editors are), I'm going to resist packing a book line beyond the next eighteen months.

Ah, now you see the problem, right? What if your proposal lands on my desk right at the time when my publishing list for the next eighteen months is already packed? Well, even if I want to publish your book, I'm going to look at my calendar, shake my head, and send it back to you with a rejection letter.

And the scapegoat I'll use is that silly old calendar that only allows twelve months in each year.

WHAT YOU CAN DO ABOUT IT...

1. Stay current on the economic news about the publishing industry.

This may not actually get you a contract, but it will help you to know when publishers are expanding or cutting titles. An e-newsletter like "PW Daily" (from *Publishers Weekly*) is an invaluable source for this kind of information. In fact, if you don't already have a free subscription to this e-newsletter, then put down this book right now and go sign up for it. Go to PublishersWeekly.com and click on the "E-Newsletters" tab at the top of the page.

Once you are getting a steady stream of publishing industry news, pay attention to layoff announcements. A cutback in personnel is almost always accompanied by a cutback in titles to be published, simply because there aren't enough people left to maintain the previous load. Also look at quarterly profit statement announcements. A company that's crowing about exceeding profit expectations also has money to spend on new books. And go ahead and check the job boards at a few companies. If one particular company is hiring several positions, that means cash flow is good and they are already planning to expand for the future.

2. Try pitching new books early in the year.

For many publishers, the new fiscal year starts January 1. Because of the spirit of a "New Year," that's also when many editors take a little time to get organized, catch up on dormant proposals, and begin laying out the pieces of their upcoming publishing plan.

You see the opportunities that arise from this kind of timing, right? If your editor's departmental budget is suddenly flush with money again, and if the change from December to January already has her thinking brightly of the future, this could be a good time to pitch her a new idea.

One warning though: You won't be the only one trying to take advantage of this situation. You'll probably have increased competition for the editor's attention in January and February, so make sure your book stands out!

3. Wait it out.

If you get a rejection because an editor's publishing list is already full for several seasons ahead, you can also try to wait it out and resubmit. Be sure to ask permission, and if it's granted, wait six months or a year and send a new query (reminding the editor that you were invited to resubmit). This is kind of a long shot, and yes, it postpones your publishing opportunities, but in cases where the editor likes you already, it can work.

{ Reason № 17 }

I Had a Fight with My Spouse and/or Children Just Before I Read Your Proposal

I know. This seems irrelevant at best, and unwarranted at worst. But it still happens, so you'd better get used to it.

This reason for rejection actually covers all the emotional and physical stresses associated with being human, and in those situations timing is everything. My reaction to your proposal is influenced if I've read it after I've just had a fight with my wife, or after I've just had to ground my son for missing his curfew, or while I'm in the middle of a long argument with my next door neighbor, or when I'm suffering from the effects of allergy season, or in the morning after a night of insomnia, or…well, you get the idea.

I remember one time I was compiling a book of short plays for teenagers. I'd put together several different authors and had cherry-picked one writer in particular—let's call her Janine—because she was one of the most creative, articulate writers I knew. Then, as I edited, I began passing them one by one to our chief creative officer for her approval.

Imagine my surprise when Janine's manuscript was sent

back to me with the note, "I didn't really enjoy this one. Let's cut it and find another."

I re-read Janine's script, laughed in all the right places, and for the life of me couldn't see why it hadn't sailed through to publication. So I took a risk and went back to my CCO to ask about it.

"Oh, you know," she said sheepishly, "we were watching our friend's pet bird while they were on vacation—and the bird died! I read this play right during the stress of trying to figure out how to tell our friends that heartbreaking news." Then she generously said, "Let me read it again this weekend, and I'll let you know what I think."

Next time I saw the play, it had a bright smiley face on it. "Love it!" my CCO said. And that was that.

Still, the fact is, Janine's script almost didn't see the light of day because my CCO read it during a time of great stress. And that's what might happen to you if an editor reads your book after just having a fight with her husband, or just hearing his daughter has wrecked the car, or whatever. Consider yourself warned.

WHAT YOU CAN DO ABOUT IT...

1. If you are religious, go ahead and pray. (If not, skip to #2 below.)

I'm not one who is opposed to the idea of God being involved in a publishing career, but if you are, then feel free to ignore this suggestion.

If you are like me, however, then I'd suggest that you go ahead and pray before you send out any query letter or proposal. Ask God to direct the path your proposal takes at a publishing house, and to bring it to the attention of people who might feel favorably toward it. Hey, what can you lose?

2. Pay attention to Facebook and Twitter.

Most editors are vain creatures, and it's likely they weren't among the "popular kids" back in their high school days. More likely, they were the mousy loners who wrote stories during study hour and hung out in some nerd's basement playing *Dungeons and Dragons* or watching classic movies at night. They probably weren't total outcasts, but they definitely weren't invited to all the cool parties either.

Fast-forward to today and these former societal outcasts have achieved a place of minor importance in the real world. And believe it or not, they often like the fictional popularity that comes with having a number of "friends" or "followers" on Facebook and Twitter. As a result, they'll probably accept your friend request on Facebook, even though they don't have a clue who you are. Same goes for Twitter followers.

What does that mean for you? Well, if you're smart, you'll pay attention when those editor types update their statuses on Twitter and Facebook. When they're updating about some personal success ("We finally finished the bathroom remodel—it looks great!"), you'll try to tag along with that good feeling by submitting an idea via email. If the editor's personal status updates are all about how the pipes burst in her home or how his whole family is worn out from cold and flu season...well, common sense would dictate that's probably not the best time to submit. After all, timing really can be everything.

3. Move on.

Hey, sometimes unfair things happen in life. You can't control the emotional state of the editor or agent who reads your work, or even when that person reads it. So if an editor rejects your outstanding book because he or she is feeling grumpy and stressed, don't waste time aggravating the situation. Move on to greener pastures—and make that editor feel even worse when you hit the bestseller list with another publisher.

{ Reason № 18 }

You Didn't Eschew Obfuscation

Reading, in my view, should be a simple, pleasant experience. Even when dealing with complex topics and weighty intellectual issues, a manuscript should never lead the reader toward confusion or away from understanding. Unfortunately, too many writers think more about themselves than they do about the reader. They think writing is about looking smart, or presenting a superior argument to a lesser mind. These people most often remain unpublished (though some do thrive in the so-called academic category).

I like the way six-year-old Calvin describes this attitude in the classic cartoon strip *Calvin & Hobbes*. "The purpose of writing," he lectures while creating a book report titled *The Dynamics of Interbeing and Monological Imperatives in* Dick and Jane, "is to inflate weak ideas, obscure poor reasoning, and inhibit clarity. With a little practice, writing can be an intimidating and impenetrable fog!"[13]

---

13   Bill Watterson, *Homicidal Psycho Jungle Cat* (Kansas City, MO: Andrews and McMeel, 1994), 62.

You see the point here, don't you? (And no, I'm not just picking on scholarly publications.) If you want to pursue a successful career in publishing, you will need to learn how to think first of your reader. This applies to nonfiction and fiction writers alike. It does no one any good if you use your writing simply as an opportunity to brandish your education or expansive vocabulary. What matters is that your audience finds your writing accessible, interesting, and worth the time spent reading it.

This is not to say, of course, that you should "dumb down" your writing at all, or that you must express yourself only in terms of the lowest common denominator on your given topic. Nor does this assume that you must be simpleminded in order to be successful as an author.

But it is to say that if you are needlessly obfuscatory, I shall expeditiously eschew your entreaty to broker financial arrangements for your forthcoming monograph. 'Nuff said.

WHAT YOU CAN DO ABOUT IT...

1. Take a lesson from *Calvin & Hobbes*.

Simplify your prose to deliver complex, elegant ideas.

Don't get caught up in the "monological imperatives in *Dick and Jane*"—that is, don't use words to *inhibit* the clarity of your thoughts, in spite of how much you like them. Instead, use your words to bring force and relevance to your ideas in the minds of your readers.

Here's a quick way to check whether you are avoiding the *Calvin & Hobbes* conundrum: Take a page (or two) of your work and simply read it out loud. Sure, you'll sound like a moron to anyone within earshot, but more importantly you'll discover with your own ears if your writing is actually readable.

Writing that is well crafted and understandable flows easily when read aloud. If you find yourself stumbling, or pausing to gather the words in your mouth, or even stopping completely because you got tripped up while reading, then mark where that happens. Those are the sections that need to be rewritten so they are clearer and more accessible to readers.

2. Eschew obfuscation.

Or rather, keep away from confusing prose.

This can deal with your specific word choices, your sentence and paragraph structure, or even the overall outline and flow of your thinking.

Believe it or not, simple, elegant writing doesn't happen by accident and it doesn't come naturally to a lot of people. More often than not, it's the uneducated author that tries to impose confusing elements onto a piece of writing. At its heart, this kind of mistake is a matter of trying to fit in, of attempting to earn respect by filling your work with things that you think others admire.

Truth is, readers admire clear, uncomplicated thinking—even in matters of great complexity and intellectual depth.

So don't ask yourself, "What can I say on this subject?" but instead ask, "What do my readers need to know to understand this subject or this story?" Then proceed accordingly.

3. Write for academic publishers.

If you absolutely can't write with everyday clarity on a subject, then you're going to have to go into academia. You'll need a few advanced degrees and a dedication to reach an isolated audience that's often out of touch with current thinking. But if this style of writing suits you, then you can succeed in this publishing category, so feel free to pursue that option.

*You Pitched Me Two Awful
Ideas in a Row*

Dear Mike,

*Look at these adorable pictures of my kitties
eating supper off china plates. Everyone should
see this! That's why I'd like you to represent my
coffee-table book filled entirely with pictures of
cats eating fancy food on expensive tableware...*
Sincerely,
Cat-Lady

• • •

Dear Cat-Lady,
No thanks.
Mike

• • •

Dear Mike,

*OK, I know you didn't like the Cats-n-China
idea, but you're going to love this one: How
about a fictional biography of my childhood?*

I can fudge a few historical papers and voilà—
I'm a survivor of the Chernobyl nuclear disas-
ter! No one would check out the stories, I'm
sure, and besides if they did the controversy
would sell more books...
Cat-Lady Survivor-Woman

• • •

Dear Cat-Lady Survivor-Woman,
No...just...no.
Mike

• • •

Dear Mike,
Hey, it's me again! Cat-Lady Survivor-Woman,
and...

• • •

Dear Cat-Lady Survivor-Woman,
NO.NO.NO.NO. Whatever it is...NO!
Mike

Yes, my examples here are a little extreme, but you get the idea.

When you're sending out pitches to editors and agents, you must remember that your name is irrevocably associated in my mind with whatever you send. If you send me one awful idea, I'll probably shrug my shoulders and move on to whatever's next in my pile. If you send me two awful ideas in a row, you've just earned yourself a brand name—and it's not a good one.

You see, for me (and for most other agents and editors), it's two strikes and you're out. After you send me two obviously unpublishable books, it's unlikely that I'll give your third book more than a glance. After all, I will instinctively consider the source. "Isn't this that strange lady who wanted to fabricate her childhood? No thanks."

Hey, your third book might be a legitimate bestseller destined to make millions, but in my eyes you'll be like "the boy who cried wolf" in the old fairy tale. I definitely won't come running when you call.

So be careful what you send me. Every word you write shapes your reputation in my eyes. And if you send me garbage twice in a row, the third time you won't even make it in the front door.

WHAT YOU CAN DO ABOUT IT...

1. Guard your reputation like a brand name.

As an agent, I'm extremely careful about what I will and won't send out to editors. My own authors will testify that I'm sometimes a big pain in the butt in that regard. If I don't think their writing is up to quality, I'll insist that they rewrite until it is. Why? Because once I attach my agency name to their writing, we are all judged the same. I can't afford for Nappaland Literary to be associated with poor writing, or else editors will stop listening when I pitch new books and new authors to them.

You need to guard your authorial reputation with the same tenacity.

Rejection in itself is no shame. But rejection because your writing is awful, your ideas are weak, or your perception of quality is woefully inaccurate—that's a death sentence in terms of a writer's career.

You must remember that *every time* you write something and send it out, those words shape an editor's perception of you and the product (writing) that you are selling. That determines your reputation in the writing community—and your reputation can often mean everything.

So make sure to guard your good name among editors and agents—and never let yourself be accused of sending out two bad proposals in a row.

2. Send to the right targets.

One reason authors are ignored by editors and agents is because they prove themselves to be irrelevant. Just as bad as sending me two awful book ideas is sending me two proposals that obviously aren't what I'd publish.

This ties into what we discussed earlier in Reason #7, but it bears repeating. If you want to get my attention, you've got to appeal to the audience I'm trying to reach. If you consistently send me books that don't do that, pretty soon I'm giving up on you. You'll get that form letter rejection before I even read your cover letter.

So take care to send your proposal to the right people—to editors and/or agents who might actually want to buy it. (Read more about this at Reason #7.)

3. Take time to become a better writer.

If you are getting rejected on the basis of the quality of your manuscripts or the appeal of your ideas, it's time to step back from the business side of writing and concentrate on the craft instead. Too many people like the idea of "being a writer" more than they like doing the work of a writer. Make sure you are someone in that second category and not the first.

Sometimes you have to admit that your writing needs to improve. Instead of whining about how no one will publish your work, learn how to create works that people *have* to publish in spite of themselves. Self-study opportunities are available in the writing reference section of your local library. You can also join a local writing group where so-called friends will gleefully rip apart your work and (hopefully) help you make it stronger. Creative writing classes are taught at just about every university and community college in the nation as well.

If you don't want to get a reputation for mediocrity—and you want to avoid being ignored on the editorial desk—do what it takes to get better. (Whining is optional.)

{ Reason № 20 }

Your Agent Pitched Me Two Awful Ideas in a Row

Honestly, this reason for rejection is kind of undeserved. After all, you have no control over your agent's bad taste—and you certainly can't tell your agent not to pitch someone else's book. But this is a case of you suffering by association.

First, you must understand the way most agents make money. It's rare for an agent to make a healthy living off only one or two clients. We agents typically get only 15 percent of whatever royalties an author's book earns. If a book is reasonably successful—say it sells 20,000 copies in its first year—an agent will likely make only $3,000 or $4,000 from that book. That's certainly not enough to support a family, let alone all the expenses associated with a literary agency. Plus, most books simply aren't "reasonably successful," and they fail to even earn back the royalty advance paid before the book was released.

So, agents make money in the same way discount stores make money: They sell in bulk. More authors mean more contracts, which means more residual royalty income, which, over time, will hopefully accumulate into a respectable annual salary. For many agents this job is mostly a numbers game, and the bigger the numbers the better.

At Nappaland Literary I've deliberately kept my author roster smaller—never more than a dozen writers on my rolls at any one time. But that's a luxury I have that most don't. Many of my colleagues routinely accept new authors regardless of how many writers are already on their rosters—and most represent fifty, sixty, even one hundred authors at once. From a numbers perspective, that's just smart business. But from a quality viewpoint (which is where many editors sit), that means you never know exactly what you're going to get next from Janice A. Agent.

If I'm an acquisitions editor working with your agent, and she sends me a crap proposal from some "exciting new voice!" she signed at a recent writer's conference, I'll probably roll my eyes and reject. If the next book she sends me is equally crap, but from a different writer on her roster, I'll begin to suspect that she doesn't really care about (or recognize) quality in writing. I'll assume she's just playing the numbers game, throwing stuff out there and hoping some of it sticks.

Once I have that perception of an agent, it's going to be hard for any book she sends me to get serious consideration. Somewhere in there, that means your book will be negatively impacted by your agent's lack of consistency in judging manuscripts.

The result? If your agent has recently sent me two unpublishable manuscripts in a row, and your book is the third one she sends me…well, I might just reject it sight unseen. Or I might be predisposed to reject it before I even give it a serious look. Either way, it's not good for you. Sorry, but that's the way it happens sometimes.

WHAT YOU CAN DO ABOUT IT...

1. Pick your agent with care.

Too many authors think that any agent is better than no agent at all. These poor souls will often sign with the first agent to show an interest, regardless of that agent's background or track record.

Don't be that desperate. Remember that your agent's reputation will become your reputation if he or she represents you. As the old knight said in *Indiana Jones and the Last Crusade*, "Choose wisely."

A few things to consider when choosing an agent:

- Who else does this agent represent, and what is their quality of writing?
- How many authors are on this agent's roster?
- What is this agent's editorial experience in publishing (i.e., has this person ever had to deal with writing quality from a hands-on editorial perspective)?
- Has this agent published books with several different publishing houses, or mostly with just a few?
- Am I impressed by the quality of writing I see in books published in association with this agent?

And no, don't think you should just ask these questions directly to a potential agent. That immediately labels you as someone who didn't do your homework before contacting an agent—and could put an agent on the defensive right at the start. This is all public information for someone willing to take the time to research the agent's website and publishing history. So do it before you contact an agency. And don't waste your time contacting an agent who doesn't pass your muster on these questions.

2. Ask your agent which times of the year tend to be "slow seasons."

The thinking here is that you want to get your proposals ready to pitch during your agent's slow seasons. Why? Because then you know that he or she isn't flooding editors with other people's book ideas. That helps your proposal to (hopefully) land on an editor's desk at a time when it can be judged on its own merits instead of being judged as part of a rainbow of books that have all been submitted within days or weeks of each other.

Also, if Joe Z. Agent is able to focus more attention on your proposal because he's not as busy with other people's books, he may also be able to give you constructive criticism that'll really help your writing stand out in comparison to others. If Joe Agent is worth his salt, that kind of attention will be invaluable to you.

3. Let the chips fall where they may.

At some point, regardless of the possibilities, you have to just recognize that you can't control everything when it comes to getting your book through the publishing committee approval process. If you've chosen your agent with care and done all you can with your manuscript, it may be best not to stress about the other factors you can't really control.

So, you know, grab a café mocha, watch a sunset through a picture window, and let your agent do whatever it is you hired her to do. Then sit back and see what happens!

{ Reason № 21 }

You Don't Have an Agent

I know I should be happy about this reason for rejection—after all, I'm a literary agent myself. The fact that most publishers won't even look at your work unless it comes to them through someone like me should make me feel giddy with the joy of an undeserved monopoly. But the author in me just chafes at this universally accepted discrimination against independent writers. It just seems wrong on a moral level—and it's often ineffective on a practical level as well.

Some big names in publishing were once slush pile refugees, including people like Mary Cahill, Philip Roth, Judith Guest, and even Anne Frank.[14] But those were the good old days, and now cost-cutting at publishing houses combined with the occasional terror threat (like the anthrax scare of 2002) means that times have changed.

So, do you really need an agent to publish books?

---

14 Katherine Rosman, "Death of the Slush Pile," *The Wall Street Journal.* (January 15, 2010).

Yes. And that stinks.

Take, for instance, the recorded message that greets aspiring authors who call Simon & Schuster with a great new idea:

"Simon & Schuster requires submissions to come to us via a literary agent due to the large volume of submissions we receive each day."

Honestly, in the great capitalist society of America, you ought to be able to approach any publisher directly with your book ideas and proposals, but that's just not the way publishing works in the twenty-first century. So you need an agent whose primary job is to build relationships with the decision-makers at the different publishing houses, and then use those relationships to approach a publisher for you, knowing that your work will at least be *considered* for publication. Without that relationship, most publishers will either fire off a rejection without ever looking at your book or, even worse, ignore your submission and never respond to it.

Here are situations when you might not need an agent: if you already have a relationship with a particular editor or publisher, if you have a friend who publishes with a particular house already and who passes on your manuscript to his or her editor, or if you self-publish a book and it sells more than 20,000 copies without the help of an established publishing company.

Otherwise, I'm sorry to report that you'll most likely need an agent before most publishers will even look at your manuscript. Are there exceptions to this rule? Sure—and I hope you're one of them. But you probably are not.

WHAT YOU CAN DO ABOUT IT...

1. Find an agent willing to take a chance on you.

This is a long, tedious effort that simply duplicates the process of pitching a book to publishers, only you pitch to people like me who may or may not be able to get you a publishing deal. The same rules apply, however, and if you find an agent willing to represent you, then your book has a much better chance of actually showing up in bookstores someday.

Best places to look for an agent are going to be in the following reference books:

- *Literary Marketplace* (published annually by R.R. Bowker; this book is expensive, so just check it out at your local library)
- *Guide to Literary Agents* (published annually by Writer's Digest Books)

2. Be your own literary agent.

This is a complicated solution to your problem, but it can work. After all, my entire agency grew out of the fact that I was representing my own work to publishers. But there are pitfalls when you are your own agent.

Sometimes a publisher will view you as illegitimate,

thinking that you are an agent in name only as a means to get your proposal past the "no unsolicited submissions" policy. I've been running Nappaland Literary Agency since 1995, and I still get this kind of treatment today. It's unfair, but it happens.

Other times a publisher will clarify their policy to exclude you anyway—meaning they'll only take submissions from New York City agents or something like that. And if you do get to the point of negotiating a contract, they will offer you less if you represent yourself because they assume you couldn't get a "real" agent to negotiate your book.

Still, if you are interested in representing yourself, you may want to check out Martin Levin's book, *Be Your Own Literary Agent*.

3. Network with agents and editors directly through writer's conferences.

The real value of a writer's conference is not in all the little workshops and keynote sessions. Sure, you might learn something at those, but those classes and lectures aren't what will get you published.

The real value of a writer's conference is that it gives you an opportunity to meet face-to-face with people who influence actual publishing decisions—editors and agents themselves. So check out Newpages.com/writing-conferences or the Shaw Guides to writer's conferences and workshops (http://writing .shawguides.com), pick out one or two that have a strong faculty, and make plans to attend, to mingle, and to get some face time with your target editor and/or agent.

Be aware, though, that a strong faculty is *not* one that's simply filled with successful authors—it's one filled with editors from recognizable publishing houses and agents from established literary agencies.

You Didn't Give Me Enough Writing Samples

When I'm shooting for a sale of your book in my publishing board, I've really only got three bullets in my gun: 1) your marketing platform, 2) your sales history/potential, and 3) the strength of your writing.

If you are a newer author, you will be inherently weak on the first two items in that list. So, I've got to really build up item number three to the point where it compensates for the weaknesses in the first two areas. That's where your writing samples come in.

In my publishing board meeting, I will highlight the artistry of your prose. I'll probably even read aloud powerful passages and pick random snatches from several pages just to make my point: *This author is AWESOME from beginning to end. Who cares if she doesn't have a TV show on cable? Her writing—and your reaction to it right now—is proof by itself that people will buy this book.*

Ah, but what if you only sent me an outline? Or maybe a summary with a sample introduction? What if you sent me the first 10,000 words of your novel, but nothing else to show that you can actually sustain a story for a full 100,000 words?

You may think you're just saving time, making your job a little easier in the face of unrealistic expectations from publishers who demand too much. But what you are really doing is sabotaging your own presentation in the publishing board meeting.

Now, just to clarify, these writing samples should be provided at the proposal stage, not at the query stage. If a publisher/agent only asks for a one-page query, you shouldn't submit the full proposal and additional writing samples until you're asked for it. But once I request your full proposal with writing samples, send me enough of your delicious prose to win over my publishing board convincingly. Don't leave me shorthanded.

Let me ask you something: If you were playing baseball and you knew you had to hit without a bat, would you step up to the plate? Of course not. But that's how you make me feel when you send me an idea without enough writing samples to demonstrate without a doubt the superior strength of your skill as an author. And then you complain when I reject your book—even though you were the one who sabotaged both of us by submitting an incomplete proposal.

I know. It takes time—a lot of time—to write up samples for a book. And since I require you to write your samples on speculation (meaning, without any guarantee of payment or a contract), you could lose both time and money by writing extensive samples for me. But…

You must remember that I didn't make the rules, and until you are successful enough to break the rules, there's only one way to avoid a rejection for this reason. You've got to give me enough stellar writing samples to accomplish what we both want to happen in publishing board: approval for your next book contract.

WHAT YOU CAN DO ABOUT IT…

1. Write enough to meet the expected requirements.

If you know that a certain amount of writing samples is required before an editor will seriously consider your book, then just buckle down and write. Don't waste time trying to prove to me that you are a deserving exception to the rule, or demanding that I overlook the requirements because you're just too busy to meet them.

Hey, nobody ever said it would be easy for you to get published. In fact, sometimes we like to make it a little hard, just to weed out the halfhearted and the weak. But you don't have to fit in either of those categories—and besides, didn't you say you wanted to be a *writer*?

Here's what you'll typically need to deliver:

- For a fiction book, you'll have to write the whole thing. Will the editor actually read the whole thing? Maybe,

maybe not. That's irrelevant. What is relevant is that rarely will any editor consider a novel from a newer author unless the whole book is written.

- For nonfiction, it's a little easier. You'll need to write 1) an annotated table of contents, 2) an introduction to your book, and 3) one sample chapter from your book (usually the first chapter, but it can be any chapter you choose).

2. Become famous enough that your writing skill doesn't matter.

We'll talk more about this in Reason #54, but for now suffice it to say that one way to avoid writing is to be famous. Publishing companies are enamored by celebrities, so much so that celebrities often don't even write their own life stories. So if you want to "be" a writer instead of doing the work of a writer, then put your writing career on hold. Pursue the life of a celebrity instead—become a rock star or a TV talk show host or a movie actor or whatever.

I know this sounds like cynical advice, and maybe it is a little bit...but I also promised to always tell you the truth in this book, and I know this pathway to authorship works. So if celebrity is within your reach or ambition, go ahead and pursue it. Once you hit the national consciousness, you'll have your pick of book publishing opportunities—and you may not even have to write a single word.

3. Review Reason #14.

Don't be lazy!

Do the work it takes to succeed, and (shocker!) you just might succeed.

{ Reason № 23 }

I've Rejected This Book Before

A few years ago I got an email proposing a book about the life story of some remarkable woman who suffered through illness and poverty, etc., before becoming a remarkable woman who still lives in illness and poverty today. Sure, somebody may be interested in reading that kind of tragic life story, but it's not the kind of book I tend to represent. I sent a rejection.

A month later, I got an email—from a different address—about that same remarkable book about that same remarkable woman. Rejected.

Then, over the course of the next year or so, I got that same book proposal—from supposedly different names and several different email addresses—at least twenty times. Every time my response was an automated rejection. I have to wonder if, after the thirteenth rejection, that author truly thought I would suddenly come to my senses and rejoice at the opportunity to represent that tired, unpublishable book. Did the author really think the fourteenth rejection wouldn't come? Or the fifteenth? Or the twentieth?

Please.

Once a book is rejected, that's pretty much it for that editor or agent. There are a few exceptions—which we'll discuss below—but generally speaking, once rejected, always rejected. If you keep resubmitting a book after it's been rejected, you've destroyed your credibility as an author with anyone who has seen your work before.

Additionally, it makes you seem desperate and dense. If you can't sell this book to me, I don't want to see it rehashed and resent to me. I want to see if you can come up with something else, something completely new that'll "wow" me out of complacency toward you. I want to see that you have grown since your last proposal, that your writing is getting better, that your market savvy is getting keener, that you really do deserve to be published.

Otherwise we're just a broken record that plays only one word: rejection…rejection…rejection…

WHAT YOU CAN DO ABOUT IT…

1. Learn to accept rejection as a natural part of your writing success.

Listen, rejection is nothing to be ashamed of in your writing career. Everybody gets rejected—and I mean *everybody*. Even J.K. Rowling's first *Harry Potter* book was rejected by twelve publishers before Bloomsbury UK finally agreed to give it a chance.[15]

---

15 Katherine Rosman, "Death of the Slush Pile," *The Wall Street Journal* (January 15, 2010).

One of my earliest royalty books was rejected a whopping twenty-two times before a tiny little publisher in Minnesota picked it up—and went on to sell more than 100,000 copies of it. In fact, my books have been rejected a few thousand times…and yet I've still managed to sell more than a million copies of books I authored or coauthored.

So if you get a rejection for a book, don't waste time trying to change an editor's mind or foolishly thinking you can "trick" an editor into accepting something he or she previously rejected. Life's too short, and you are too good, for that kind of self-defeating behavior. Accept the rejection as another step on your way to success, and move on.

2. Be aware of the exceptions to the "no resubmits" rule—but use them sparingly.

There are *rare* occasions when it is acceptable to resubmit a manuscript that's been rejected. Generally speaking, you should never resubmit a rejected proposal. But, just in case the opportunity arises for you, here are the exceptions to this rule:

- The editor or agent suggests revisions and invites you to resubmit after changes have been made. One caveat, though: Never do more than one round of revisions for an editor in this situation. If the editor doesn't like your book after you've tailored it to his or her tastes a first time, it's unlikely to pass muster the next time.

- The editor or agent says her current load is full but she'd be open to taking another look in six months or something. This one's easy. Wait six months and resubmit, reminding the editor that she requested the resubmission.

- There's a change in the editorial staff and you know your book never made it to committee last time. Hey, if the rejecting editor leaves and no one else has seen your book, it means it's a new proposal for the new editorial team. In this case, simply submit again as if for the first time.

3. Write something new.

So your book got rejected. So what? If you're as talented and intelligent as I think you are, then simply shrug it off and start on something new. Take charge of your own success by giving yourself a brand-new opportunity with a brand-new book.

And if that gets rejected too…well, so what? As long as you're willing to try again, you're never without opportunities.

{ Reason № 24 }

You Are Clueless about Copyright Law

In 1951, J.D. Salinger published what has become a classic American novel, *The Catcher in the Rye*—a book that's sold more than 35 million copies to date. In early 2009, Swedish author Fredrik Colting (writing under the pen name "J.D. California") self-published his first novel through his own small publishing house. It was titled *60 Years Later: Coming through the Rye.*[16]

Colting's book borrowed its lead character, Holden Caulfield, from Mr. Salinger's original, imagining what might happen to this legendary antihero at age seventy-six. (Not surprisingly, it was pretty similar to what happened to him at sixteen.) Colting even advertised his new book as "a marvelous sequel to one of our most beloved classics."

The problem? J.D. Salinger alone owns the copyright to the character of Holden Caulfield, and only he has the sole and exclusive right to publish any sequels to *The Catcher in the*

---

16 "John David California," *Wikipedia* (March 12, 2010).

Rye. No one else. The only exceptions would be in the case of parody or distinct literary criticism on the original work. When Mr. Salinger heard of "J.D. California" and the unauthorized sequel to his book, he objected with great gusto.

It was not surprising, then, that in July 2009 a U.S. District Court barred publication of Colting's book in the United States on grounds of copyright infringement.[17] What was surprising is that Fredrik Colting was surprised. He appeared blissfully unaware that he was violating basic copyright law.

And that's where you come in.

Unfortunately, a great number of aspiring writers appear to share Mr. Colting's disregard for copyright ownership. Intellectual property laws seem to be nothing more than a minor nuisance for lawyers to worry about. As a result, copyright issues are often ignored or misapplied in an effort to achieve quick success in publishing.

I know of authors who thought nothing of simply copying blocks of text off Martha Stewart's website and pasting them right into their own manuscripts. Another editor I know actually lost his job when he trusted one of his authors had written what he'd said he'd written. Turned out that author had simply appropriated material from a *Chicken Soup for the Soul* book, blissfully unaware that he was violating copyright law by doing that. And the list goes on.

---

17 Larry Neumeister, "60 Years Later Blocked: Judge Says No To Salinger Spinoff," *Huffington Post* online (July 1, 2009).

So here's the deal: If you send me your next great idea, and it's based on someone else's original idea (a sequel to *Star Wars*, anyone?), or if I see that you haven't properly documented your sources, or if it's apparent that you are mistake-prone when dealing with copyright issues...well, I'm going to reject your book. I can't afford to face the legal liabilities that might be incurred because you are ignorant of the law.

WHAT YOU CAN DO ABOUT IT...

1. Become an expert on copyright law.

The simple fact is that if you intend to profit from intellectual property (your writing), you'd better know how the law governs your rights to that property.

For instance, did you know that your copyright benefits are actually a constitutional right (up there with freedom of speech and the abolition of slavery)? They are guaranteed by Article 8, Section 8 of the U.S. Constitution. And did you know that you don't even have to publish or affix a copyright notice on your work for it to be copyrighted? In fact, putting a copyright notice on your book proposal immediately shows you are a rank amateur and someone I will have to educate if I sign you to a contract. As soon as you put your words into "fixed form" (such as on paper, in a computer file, or even on an audio recording), they are solely and completely yours.

These are the simplest principles of copyright ownership. It would be wise for you to become an expert on the rest. Here are a few resources to help you do that:

- *Intellectual Property* by Roger E. Schechter and John R. Thomas (highly recommended)
- *Kirsch's Handbook of Publishing Law* by Jonathan Kirsch
- *The Public Domain* by Stephen Fishman
- U.S. Copyright Office: www.copyright.gov

2. Create your own success.

Seriously, you don't need to depend on someone else's writing or ideas or characters or universes or whatever. You are certainly capable of creating success on your own, without having to rip off someone else's material. So just do that. Don't waste your time trying to re-create what someone else has already created. Demand more of yourself. You'll be pleased with the result.

3. Understand the nuances of parody and "unauthorized" publishing.

Yes, it's true that there are certain instances when you can legally appropriate material from another author and use it to create something of your own. The issues typically deal with definitions of "parody," "criticism and commentary," and "transformative results." These exceptions are why you see "unauthorized" books about your favorite TV shows, or even a goofy film like *Family Guy Presents: Something Something Something Dark Side*.

However—and this is important—an attempt at parody or "unauthorized" publishing can easily cross the line into copyright infringement, so *you must know what you are doing*. What's more, you must be able to clearly defend yourself in a court of law. If you intend to pursue parody or unauthorized publishing, make sure you understand the nuances of those exceptions in the law. And make sure you can satisfactorily explain for an editor how they apply to your manuscript.

This subject is too complex to deal with adequately here, so check out the copyright references listed in #1 above for more details.

{ Reason № 25 }

Your Book Is Boring

There's no law against writing a boring book…but there ought to be.

Whether you're writing fiction or nonfiction, a children's picture book or a teen romance, a psychology textbook or a Mediterranean cookbook, if you bore me I will reject you.

Unfortunately for you, I have a very short attention span—and most agents and editors are just like me. We blame it on the fact that we're very busy, our time always seems crunched, etc., etc. But the truth is just that our kind bores easily. Very little of what we read is new, and without even thinking we're automatically dissecting your paragraph structure, the rhythm of your writing, and our emotional reaction to your words.

You've got to "wow" us, and keep wowing us from beginning to end. Otherwise you'll never keep our attention.

No, that doesn't mean you have to have explosions and death-defying stunts on every page. But it does mean there should be some kind of "wow" factor that engages the reader—and then keeps the reader going through the book. This can be in the way you create curiosity in the reader, or in the deft characterizations you deliver, or in the thoughtful and compelling reasoning of your ideas, and so on.

Remember, though, whatever you write, the "wow" should be easy to see. Otherwise, it'll only take me about sixty seconds (or less) to get bored and reject your book.

WHAT YOU CAN DO ABOUT IT...
1. Start well.

Bestselling novelist Harlan Ellison says, "An otherwise excellent story can find itself being stuffed back into an SASE and being dropkicked into the mail chute because it had a slow, an obscure, a confusing, or redundant opening section."[18] And Mr. Ellison is right.

If you intend to avoid writing a boring book, the first step is to avoid writing a boring beginning to your book (see Reason #15 for more on this). Or, to look at it another way, if you *wanted* to write a boring book, you'd do the following:

Fill your opening pages with backstory and exposition. Spend awhile making sure I get all the background on your characters and their setting. Tell me all about their hair color, the number of trees in their yards, where their cousins live, and so on. Make me wade through all that irrelevant stuff before I can finally appreciate your plot.

---

18 Harlan Ellison, as quoted by Robert Bly in *88 Money-Making Writing Jobs*, (Naperville, IL: Sourcebooks, 2009), 257.

Of course, I'll reject you…but at least you can boast about how boring your writing is, right?

2. Show, don't tell.

This is a basic writing instruction, especially for fiction authors. The point is this: don't spend time telling me something when you can engage me with a word picture or mental image of that thing instead.

For instance, you could *tell* me: "Martin smoked a lot every day." Of course, that would be booor-ring. Or you could *show* me Martin's habit: "Perched on the corner of Martin's desk was a faded ash tray, filled to the edges with spent cigarette butts and surrounded by crumpled, empty packs of Chesterfields." The first description *tells* me about Martin, but the second delivers a visual image that *shows* me Martin's habit without ever having to say, "Martin smokes a lot."

The problem with *telling* in a manuscript is that it most often is an interruptive technique. It actually stops the story in order to lecture the reader on some fact or tidbit of information.

Think for a minute about what happens when you watch TV. Do you ever enjoy it when your favorite show stops completely to lecture you with a PSA about meth abuse, or when your football game grinds to a halt so some automotive company can tell you how tough their trucks are? As important as education about meth abuse is, and as true as it may be that some company makes tough trucks, no one likes being interrupted to hear about those things. Likewise, telling interrupts the reader as he or she is enjoying your story. Do it too often, and your reader will eventually get bored and give up.

3. Avoid unnecessary repetition.

Veteran editors Renni Browne and Dave King observe, "Most authors already know to edit out places where they have literally repeated a word or phrase. But the repetition of an *effect* can be just as problematic. Whether it's two sentences that convey the same information, two paragraphs that establish the same personality trait, or two characters who fill the same role in the plot, repetition can dissipate your writing and rob it of its power."[19]

I am tempted to expand on this more, but after reading again the comments of the esteemed Browne and King, I realize that anything I say now will simply be a repeat of their excellent advice! So, suffice it to say that unnecessary repetition in a manuscript is boring—don't do it.

---

19 Renni Browne and Dave King, *Self-Editing for Fiction Writers* (New York: Quill/HarperResource, 1993, 1994, 2001), 129–130.

{ Reason № 26 }

You Took the D-Train

D-Train writing is a concept I learned from the inimitable Lawrence Block. It's related to Reason #25, and now that I know what it is, I can never again read a book that uses it within its pages—let alone pitch it to a publisher.

So take this to heart, dear reader: *Never take the D-Train when you write.*

Ah, you say, what exactly is the D-Train? It's a visual image that reminds us of the power of transitions in writing. It's what happens when an author spends too much time dawdling between one scene to the next in fiction, or from one thought to the next in nonfiction. It was inspired from a rather long, detailed passage Mr. Block once wrote about a character who left his Manhattan apartment and took a subway to Harlem.

As Block explained it in his fabulous book, *Telling Lies for Fun and Profit*, "I was telling my readers considerably more than they cared or needed to know about something that was neither germane to my story nor interesting in and of itself—i.e., the subway system of the city of New York."[20]

Block's point is this: Transitions matter—and mundane, convoluted attempts to get from one place to another in a manuscript are always hard to accept. "Film and television techniques have made readers more sophisticated," he says. "We don't have to have things spelled out for us as thoroughly as we once did."[21] What's more, a cluttered transition reveals muddled thinking and an aimless progression in a writer's prose. Readers won't put up with that for very long—and they shouldn't have to.

Poor transitions also label you immediately as a novice, and to be honest, that means more work for me. If I have to teach you how to write in order to be successful representing your book, I'm going to think twice before signing you to my agency. Same goes for an editor and a publishing house.

So pay close attention to transitions as you write. And never, never take the D-Train.

WHAT YOU CAN DO ABOUT IT...
1. Read *Telling Lies for Fun and Profit*.
Seriously. Go get it.

Lawrence Block wrote this book two decades ago, and

---

20 Lawrence Block, *Telling Lies for Fun and Profit* (New York: Quill/William Morrow, 1981, 1994), 150.

21 Block, 151.

there's a reason why it's still in print. Mr. Block is one of the few people out there who can actually take a story apart into all its little pieces and then put it back together in such a way that it's better than it was to start. The fact that he's willing to share that skill with you and me is our good luck.

Telling Lies for Fun and Profit is always the book I recommend first at any writer's conference. And people who read it are always better writers afterward. If you buy this book only to get the chapter called "Don't Take the D-Train," your money will have been well spent.

2. Pay attention to your transitions.

"Transitions are tricky," Block says. "Transitions continue to demand that the writer make a choice, deliberate or intuitive, as to just how and where he will interrupt the narrative action and how and where he will pick it up again."[22]

For that reason, transitions deserve more than just your passing attention. First, as you write, keep in mind what the reader needs and wants to hear. If you find yourself writing simply to get from point A to point B, reevaluate what you're doing. If there's nothing in that passage that's required for the larger story you are telling, it may be that you've accidentally slipped onto the platform of the D-Train.

Next, when you've finished, read your manuscript with a

---

22   Block, 154.

deliberate eye toward transitions. Identify them in your writing, and subject them to intense scrutiny. Ask yourself: "Does this transition move the story forward, or stop the story in its tracks? Does this transition effectively, and quickly, get from A to B? Or does it dawdle and meander? Are these words absolutely necessary to my story…or not?"

If you are careful about the way you scrutinize your transitions, chances are you'll avoid riding the D-Train—and that means you just might avoid rejection as well.

3. Read other writers, and highlight their transition passages.

Go out to a used bookstore and pick up a few cheap copies of your favorite books. And while you're at the checkout counter, add a yellow highlighter to your purchase. Then take them all home and start reading.

Every time you see a transition passage that you think is effective at avoiding the D-Train, go ahead and highlight that section. Be aware that you'll have to pay attention to see these, because good authors are adept at making their transitions almost invisible! Afterward, flip through your books and compare the passages that you highlighted. What do they have in common? What makes them successful? What techniques do you see that you can adapt and use for your own nefarious purposes?

The best writing teachers are always other writers, so use

them to help you become a pro at writing transitions in your own books. Who knows? Someday, some aspiring author may be highlighting passages of your books, looking for new ways to avoid the D-Train.

Your Project Is Unoriginal

As I write this book, Stephenie Meyer's *Twilight* series dominates pop culture, with books and movies and even vampire makeup styles raking in lots of money.

As such, *Twilight* has created a "brandwagon" of sorts that many people are trying to use to cash in a little bit (for more on "brandwagons," see Reason #55 later in this book). Now, I have no qualms about profiting from a popular trend—in fact, I often recommend it. But today I'm looking at a proposal I got recently from a pastor/author:

"It's *Twilight* for Christian teens!" he is telling me proudly. Apparently he thinks I'll be impressed by his ability to copycat another author's idea.

I'm not.

In fact, I'm bored by it. You see, his pitch sounds like everybody else who wants to write teen fiction right now, and enough of those have come across my desk to make me tired of the whole idea.

Do you know why *Twilight* was published, and why it was successful?

It was *original*. The author took elements of several genres—romance, horror, mythology—and combined them into something unique and compelling. That was hard for a publisher to resist, even when Stephenie Meyer was just another unknown writer with dreams of publishing a book or two.

You must remember, when you're pitching new books to me and my colleagues, we see hundreds (sometimes thousands) of book proposals every year. When you sift through that many manuscripts, you quickly realize there aren't many new ideas out there. The ones that stand out aren't books that copycat others in style or content. What gets my attention are books that deliver something original to an established audience.

Hey, Stephenie Meyer already wrote *Twilight*. There's no need for you to try to do that job again, regardless of your particular slant on the topic. And if all you really have to offer me is just another unoriginal idea, then don't expect me to give you the novelty of accepting your book.

WHAT YOU CAN DO ABOUT IT...

1. Go with the fourth idea.

Early in my publishing career, I took a low-level editorial job at a midsize publishing house. My boss there, Steve Parolini, was one of those rare guys who both challenged and encouraged you toward excellence. He had a profound impact on my career as a whole, and on my ability to be successful in publishing.

Part of my editorial responsibilities included writing manuscripts from time to time. I remember once he sent a manuscript back to me. Somehow, even though he expected me to do a complete rewrite, he was so tactful and helpful that I actually thanked him for tearing my writing to shreds. The one thing I remember from that session, though, was this advice he gave me:

"Take time to brainstorm your three absolute best ideas. Then go with your fourth idea."

What he was telling me was that I should never settle for the obvious; I should always stretch myself to create something original and new in my writing.

So now I share that same advice with you: Avoid the easily rejected curse of unoriginality. Come up with your three best ideas…then go with your fourth.

2. Exercise your creative muscles.

Contrary to popular opinion, creativity is as much a learned skill as it is an innate one. So make sure your creative muscles remain active and in good health. Spend time in deliberate pursuit of creative endeavors—stretch yourself in ways that have nothing to do with writing, and you'll see that creative effort reflected in the quality of your ideas.

For instance, try driving home from work by a different route one day. Or sample an ice cream flavor you've never heard of before. Unpack your groceries according to color. Sort your closet by what the ten-year-old version of you would've liked best. Draw on a napkin. Invent a bed-making device. The only limit is your imagination! And if your imagination is in good working order, then you're well on your way to creating an original idea that somebody like me just might want to publish.

3. Ask yourself: "What would make [insert author name] want to copycat me?"

The most flattering thing one author can say about another's work is, "I wish I'd written that." So pick your favorite author and imagine what you can create that might make that person jealous enough to say to friends, "I wish I'd written that guy's book."

One of my authors, Sharon Carter Rogers, always imagines that Stephen King is going to read her novels. Because of that, she has a "King Rule" in her writing. If she thinks Stephen King won't be impressed, she doesn't write it. To date, Mr. King has not yet read a Sharon Carter Rogers book—but at least she's ready, just in case!

That kind of attitude can help you overcome the blahs of unoriginality—so keep it in mind next time you are creating a brand-new masterpiece of modern literature.

{ Reason № 28 }

Your Cover Letter Was Too Long

Yes, I know, this seems like a petty reason to reject a book. After all, you've been taught by "experts" that a cover letter has to include a number of certain things, right?

Everybody knows that a cover letter is supposed to have a strong, attention-grabbing opener. It should have a summary of your proposed book. It should list your qualifications for writing the book, and describe any unique marketing opportunities you bring to the table. It should include a note as to whether yours is an exclusive or simultaneous submission, and whether you've got artwork available to use. It should tell who the audience is and why they'll buy. It should blah blah *blah blah.*

I'm going to tell you the truth: most of that advice is hooey.

It's rare that an experienced editor actually reads your cover letter anyway. We're more interested in the book itself than we are in your puffery about it. And besides, most of that information above should be included in the proposal section for your book. Why duplicate it in the cover letter?

Here's the risk that you take with a long cover letter: If you bore me too soon (see Reason #25), I'll probably reject your book before I even get to your manuscript. Also, letter writing is a different skill than, say, novel writing or children's book writing or even nonfiction writing. But I'll prejudge your skill in all those categories by my first impression of the cover letter you sent me.

Your cover letter really should just be an introduction, along with a short request for consideration of your book's publishing potential. But if your letter reveals you to be a "Long Talker"—that is, someone who doesn't know when to shut up—well, chances are good that I'll cut you off with a letter of my own. A rejection letter.

WHAT YOU CAN DO ABOUT IT...

1. Get in the door, then get out of the way.

When you send me a cover letter, here's all I really need to see: 1) your contact info, 2) a request that I consider publishing your book, 3) a brief (two sentences max) description of why you are the ideal author for me, 4) a brief summary of why readers will want to buy your book.

Give me that info, and then get out of the way. Tell me if I have questions or need more info, that I should feel free to dive into your proposal itself, where I'll find all the additional details I want—and then some. Make me curious to find out what I'm missing if I don't read your full proposal.

After all, what would you enjoy more, reading *about* a book—or reading the book itself?

2. Never, don't ever, let your cover letter be longer than one page.

Regardless of what you include in your cover letter, it's unwise to ever let it go past the one-page mark in length. Otherwise it won't get read.

When an editor or an agent gets a two- or four-page cover letter, the best you can expect is that he or she will skim to the end. We just can't afford to take the time to read these preliminary materials in detail until after we've decided that we want to pursue your book. Otherwise we'd never get ahead of the workload on our desks. (And honestly, a lot of editors never do accomplish that anyway.) As for me, when I get a long cover letter, I typically read the first paragraph and the last, and skip everything in the middle.

So be careful not to sabotage yourself with a cover letter. Keep it to one page, and it might actually get read.

3. Beef up your proposal so you can cut down your cover letter.

I hear what you are saying to me. "Mike, you're giving me a double standard here! In this book you're telling me that all kinds of things are absolutely essential to tell an editor about my book—but now you're telling me to keep my mouth shut.

What's up with you?"

OK, I understand that this advice might be frustrating and possibly confusing. But what we're talking about here are priorities. The number one priority of your cover letter is simply to get the editor to read your manuscript. That's it. So do what it takes to get that to happen, and keep your cover letter's focus there.

All that other info you need to include? It belongs in the proposal section of your submission package. That's where you can talk in detail about your unique credentials, the mass audience appeal of your book, the special marketing opportunities for your book, and so on.

Remember, your proposal section can be as long, and as detailed, as you want it to be. So beef up that section—and keep your cover letter lean and focused.

{ Reason № 29 }

You Stink at Grammar and Spelling

In 1631 Robert Barker and Martin Lucas were the royal printers in London. Imagine their pride when, by order of King Charles I himself, they were commissioned to publish a new edition of the King James English version of the Bible.

All went well for Barker and Lucas, and their publication of the Scriptures was considered a general success, until...

About a year later, it was discovered that a compositor error had omitted a single, tiny little word ("not") from Exodus 20:14. The result of that teensy error in sentence structure? God's 7th Commandment now read: "Thou shalt commit adultery."

Barker and Lucas were publicly reprimanded, fined what was then an enormous sum, and stripped of their printing license.[23]

Still, Barker and Lucas were in good company. Some twenty years earlier, in 1611, the first edition of the King James Bible also contained a muff. A reference in Ruth 3:15 was

---

23 "Wicked Bible," *Wikipedia* (May 8, 2010).

inadvertently misspelled, which caused the biblical heroine to be identified "he" instead of "she."[24]

Why do I tell you these stories? Because I want you to understand that words have meaning and consequence.

If your words are garbled, misspelled, grammatically challenged, omitted, duplicated, misused, or otherwise incoherent, your meaning is lost. The consequence of that kind of presentation is that I will be both frustrated by you and doubtful of your credibility as an author.

Hey, you claim to be an author, but you can't even string together a coherent sentence? Very funny joke. But I'm not laughing.

Yes, a certain amount of typographical error is to be expected in any lengthy piece of writing, your book proposal included. But if I begin to see more than just a few inadvertent typos or even one glaring error in the way you use our language, your proposal won't last very long in my hands. It'll be rjectd.

Excuse me. I mean *rejected*.

WHAT YOU CAN DO ABOUT IT...

1. Memorize this website address: Dictionary.com.

I'm amazed how many authors simply don't double-check when they use unfamiliar words. On more than one occasion,

---

24 "One of the most important volumes in the Western world," The Manhattan Rare Book Company website, www.theworldsgreatbooks .com/king_james_he_bible.htm.

I've actually sat with an author, looking at a manuscript, and asked, "What does this word mean?" My question is always sincere—if I don't know something, I'm the kind of guy who isn't embarrassed to ask about it. Too many times the author has looked blankly at me and either stumbled through a guess at the meaning or simply said, "I don't know exactly."

Crazy. Why give away precious real estate in your manuscript to a word whose meaning is unsure to you? Look, words are more than just tools. They are the gems you use to decorate the jewelry of your prose. Guard them. Study them. Know them.

And visit Dictionary.com for instant help or even just to expand your vocabulary. When it's this easy, you have no excuse for word abuse.

2. Keep this book next to your computer: *The Pocket Wadsworth Handbook*.

You may feel like an uneducated high schooler when you buy this book, but it's worth it. *The Pocket Wadsworth Handbook* by Laurie G. Kirszner and Stephen R. Mandell contains—in easily accessible, clearly organized sections—all the grammar and spelling rules you and I should have memorized before going to the senior prom.

I actually discovered this book when I was teaching English composition at a local university. So many of my students had graduated from high school without basic grammar skills that I was constantly frustrated by having to explain again what they should have already known. Finally, I required every student to buy this book, and then I just started marking their papers with notes for them to study certain pages from it.

Now, don't tell my students this, but along the way I discovered I didn't know as much as I thought I did about grammar and spelling! So I kept this book, and I still use it as a reference whenever I'm unsure of whether to use "lay" or "lie," or when it's appropriate to use a semicolon. I'd recommend you keep a copy nearby as well.

3. Swallow your arrogance.

Some writers are almost haughty about their grammar and spelling skills—or dismissive of their lack of expertise in those areas. Those people deserve the rejections they receive. Don't be one of them.

Instead, when you're done writing, assume the worst. Recognize that even your best effort is going to be pockmarked with errors and unintentional corruptions. Swallow your pride and take steps to eliminate (as much as you can) the mistakes you know are there. Here's a process I use that, while not perfect, certainly helps:

1. Spell- and grammar-check. Use the basic spell-check function in your software to catch obvious errors.
2. Re-read the manuscript word for word, beginning to end, on your computer. (I'm always amazed at how

many stupid mistakes this reveals, like words left out of sentences, cut-and-paste casualties, and confusing word choices.)

3. Spell- and grammar-check again.

4. Print hard copy and read it, word for word, beginning to end, marking corrections with a pen. (Again, there are always obvious errors that I should have caught earlier when I do this!)

5. Make corrections on the computer file. Spell-check and grammar-check again.

6. Find a friend or family member to read the manuscript and mark errors.

7. Make corrections…and pray you caught everything!

You Didn't Give Me a Complete Proposal

Imagine that you and I are professional bakers. We've got a recipe for chocolate-raspberry muffins that our customers simply love, and so we agree to work together to bring those to market. I promise to do the actual cooking, the messy measuring and mixing work in the kitchen. You promise to supply the ingredients needed to make our delicious muffins.

Now, you and I both know that this recipe requires chocolate chips, eggs, flour, milk, baking soda, salt, and fresh raspberries. So it's not unreasonable for me to expect you to bring those things to the kitchen. But what if you show up with a lumpy bag containing only chocolate chips and eggs?

Well, I could make chocolate scrambled eggs...but not chocolate-raspberry muffins.

Or what if you delivered to me baking soda, salt, chocolate, and raspberries, but left out the flour and milk? Well, again, without the complete ingredients I simply can't make the full recipe.

Unfortunately, this is the way some authors view their proposal submissions. They send the parts they like (chocolate!

raspberries!), and either ignore the need for other necessities in the "contract approval recipe," or provide cheap, poorly made ingredients that simply can't stand in for the quality required in baking.

Please understand this: If you want me to cook with you in the publisher's symbolic kitchen, you've got to give me all the ingredients I need to have success with the publishing recipe. The place to do that is in your proposal.

Typically speaking, every book pitch you send out should include the following elements:

- compelling title and subtitle
- short (one paragraph) at-a-glance summary of the book's content
- short summary of your author bio/credentials
- short description of series potential (mostly for fiction only)
- manuscript details (such as word count, completion time frame, and shelving category)
- clear identification of your book's primary target audience, along with potential secondary audiences that could add on sales
- clear, compelling statements of reader benefits (that could be used in marketing copy)
- competitive analysis of books like yours that are already on the market

- annotated table of contents, with chapter-by-chapter content summaries (for nonfiction)
- plot summary (for fiction books; best to keep this at around 500 to 1,000 words)
- compelling writing samples (introduction and at least one full chapter for nonfiction; full manuscript for fiction)

There are also additional elements you can add to your proposal that are helpful—such as a list of potential endorsers, a mock cover design, PR possibilities, or even a mock advertising piece—but those are not essential. The things that are essential are the bulleted items above. If you send me a proposal without these ingredients, chances are good I'll view it as incomplete—and reject your book.

WHAT YOU CAN DO ABOUT IT...

1. Don't omit anything an editor expects.

Before today you might have been able to plead ignorance when it came to preparing your book proposals. Ah, but with knowledge comes responsibility. Now that you know what I have to have to succeed with your proposal, you have no excuse.

So don't send a proposal unless it's complete. If that means you have to take extra time or postpone your submission schedule, so be it. You'll do better by including everything I need anyway, so it'll be time well spent.

2. Don't do a shoddy job on anything my publishing board will see.

Some authors live by the rule that "anything is better than nothing" or "good enough is good enough." Unfortunately, neither of those philosophies is true.

The only thing worse than sending me an incomplete proposal is sending me complete crap in your proposal. Your proposal should reflect clear, competent thinking that is reinforced by the superb samples of your writing. If you've rushed through your competitive analysis, or don't actually understand how to articulate reader benefits in a compelling way, you've wasted what little time you spent on those things.

Remember, good enough is never good enough. I've got to show your work to my publishing committee and use it to convince them to spend money on your book. So make sure you submit only your best, from beginning to end.

3. Don't pitch to me until you are absolutely sure you've got all the ingredients I need to succeed with your proposal.

Before you send me your work, the one gift you have is time. As long as my company is in business, I'll be considering book proposals—yours included. So take the time you need to prepare a complete, effective proposal package before you send it to me.

After all, you're only going to get one chance for this book to make a good impression on me. So be sure to make it count.

{ Reason № 31 }

Bottom Line—You Didn't Do Enough of My Job for Me

Yes, this is a "catchall" reason for editorial rejection, and one that's not often articulated in publishing circles simply because it makes us agents and editors look like lazy loafers in our work. Obviously agents and editors work hard—in our industry it's required for success. At the same time, we all hate doing extra work.

As I mentioned in the introduction (and despite the arrogance with which we typically carry ourselves), the fact is when it comes to your book we editors are advocates at best and cheap salespeople at worst. In order to secure a contract for you, we've literally got to sell your idea to the people who have the power over the corporate checkbook.

If you've ever had to work in retail, you know what this is like—and how difficult it can be to overcome the obstinacy of a miser and his money. As a result, we've got what seems like a million little details to attend to, all with the hopes that our diligence in preparation for a publishing board presentation will result in successfully securing a contract for your book.

Meanwhile, we're also in the middle of editing several other books on our schedule, dealing with a temperamental author or two, preparing to present at a sales conference for books we acquired a year or two ago that are just now reaching the public, sifting through a billion other book proposals, answering tedious emails, solving problems that unexpectedly arise during production, and...well, you get the idea.

What that means for you is that, both on an emotional and intellectual level, I prejudge your proposal based on the amount of new work I expect it will make for me.

If I like your book, but realize I'm going to have to teach you how to organize your thoughts, or how to write dialogue, or whatever, I'll usually reject. If I see that your competitive analysis is nonexistent or weak, that means I'm going to have to do it for you if I want to publish your book. But I'm already overwhelmed in my work; I'm just not going to take the time for that. I'll reject you instead. Same goes for titling, author platform summaries, and anything else that's actually part of my job—but which I'm hoping you've already done for me.

Bottom line, editorially speaking?

Your best chance to avoid rejection is to do as much of my job for me as possible, and show it in your proposal. After all, I do hate taking on extra work.

WHAT YOU CAN DO ABOUT IT...

1. Review Reason #30.

If your proposal is complete, you're already a step ahead of 90 percent of the other authors pitching books to me this week. So use the information there to make sure you've already done all the basics of my job before you send me your book.

2. Become familiar with my job responsibilities.

Don't simply assume you know what an editor does. Most likely, you don't have a clue as to all the little frustrations that fill our days. So try to find out. Read career books on editorial jobs. Check out editorial jobs on Monster.com or CareerBuilder.com, and study the specific responsibilities and qualifications listed in those job descriptions. If possible, ask to be allowed to "shadow" an editor for a day at a publishing company, magazine office, or newspaper headquarters in your local area. (Bring along your son or daughter and pretend it's an "educational field trip" for your children.)

The point is, once you know what mundane tasks fill up my day, you can tailor your proposal to complete them for me. Then when I look at your book, I'll rejoice that it makes my job easy for once—and will advocate enthusiastically for your book as a result.

3. Remember that, when it comes to securing a contract for your book, my primary job is as your salesperson.

Think of me as someone you're hiring to effectively present your book to my publishing board. Now, you're not going to just slap a few pages in my hand and send me off to close the sale. No, if you really want me to make those customers buy, you're going to take time to immerse me in a thorough training about the features and benefits of your product (your book), to suggest real-world sales strategies I can use with my customers, and to give me every tool you can think of to help me succeed.

After all, you only succeed if I do.

So when you prepare your proposal pitch and writing samples, make sure you give me everything I need to be the best salesperson your book could possibly have.

{ **Part Two** }

Marketing Reasons for Rejection

{ Reason № 32 }

You Have No Idea What It Means to Market a Book

In this context I'm using the word "market" synonymously with the word "promote." Yes, I know that in business school they teach you the supposed "Four Ps of Marketing" ("product, price, place, and promotion"), but for your purposes the primary marketing concern is that last "P"—promotion. So let's ignore those other Ps and focus on what's important.

If you want to publish a book, you have to help my marketing VP succeed in her job of promoting that book. If you don't know what that means, or if you have an overly simplistic/inaccurate view of what it takes to market a book, then you've already set yourself up for failure.

I have a friend who partnered with another friend to create and self-publish a very worthwhile media product. During the time they were creating that product, they spoke enthusiastically about how they'd set a goal of selling 50,000 copies soon after publication. I was impressed, so I asked them, "How will you market this product?"

"Well, we're going to have a website," one said.

I nodded, waiting.

Finally they said, "And we'll figure out the rest when the time comes."

That was it. That was their marketing plan. That was how they intended to spread the word to hundreds of thousands of potential buyers. Put up a website. And figure out the rest later. Needless to say, they fell *far* short of their goal.

Unfortunately, too many authors think that marketing a book is something for someone else (i.e., the publisher) to worry about. And honestly, it should be—an author ought to just write, right? But in today's publishing climate, that's not the way it works.

When your book comes up for review at publishing board, my marketing VP is going to want to know that you'll be a real partner in the promotional efforts—not simply dead weight. To my VP, if you have no idea what it takes to market your own book, then you don't deserve to be published.

WHAT YOU CAN DO ABOUT IT...

1. Study the basics of book promotion. Duh.

OK, we all know about the "big" promotional vehicles: TV commercials, radio spots, infomercials, magazine ads, newspapers, movies, product placement, and so on. Truth is, your book will get none of that.

In reality, your book will probably get:

- a spot in the corporate catalog
- a sell-sheet that's shown to bookstore buyers
- a press release (maybe)
- advance Reader Copies (ARCs) sent to basic media outlets prior to publication (maybe)
- a certain number of "Influencer Copies"—that is, a certain number of books that you can direct the publisher to mail for free to people you know who are considered "influential"

That's about it—but honestly, a book can succeed with that as the starting point. So your job is to understand what goes into creating those things and then providing that material in your proposal.

A helpful resource for you in that effort is *Publicize Your Book!* by Jacqueline Deval, so be sure to check that out.

2. Learn to speak in terms of benefits.

As an advertising copywriter myself, this is always what makes the difference between getting paid quickly or having to do a rewrite. You see, marketing VPs got to where they are by being able to tell readers, in clear, compelling language, exactly why they'll *benefit* from buying certain books. So if you want to appeal to a marketer, you'll need to learn how to speak about your book in terms of its benefits.

We'll talk about this in more detail in Reason #34, but for

now try this: When your manuscript is done, take a good hard look at it and ask, "What specific *benefits* does this book give a reader?" Make a list, and make it clear and compelling. Then speak in those terms as much as possible when you're writing up your proposal package.

Make your benefits obvious and you'll grab a marketing VP's attention.

3. Create key marketing phrases to go with your book.

Think about things like

- What's the one-sentence "hook" that'll make people curious enough to read your book?
- What are the "felt needs" a reader has that'll prompt him or her to be attracted to your book?
- What are the unique features of your book—and why are they important to your reader?
- What's an attention-grabbing headline that could be used on the back cover of your book?

Then craft one-sentence, sound-bite-style phrases that can be used for each of those questions above. Gauge them for impact, clarity, conciseness, and emotion. Then, when you've got something you think could be plugged right into use for the promotion of your book, add a section to your proposal that showcases them for the marketing VP.

{ Reason № 33 }

You Have No Legitimate Means for Promoting a Book

What we're talking about here is commonly referred to as "author platform." That is, the author's unique ability to spread the word about his or her upcoming book.

Best friends with Oprah Winfrey and can promise she'll mention your book on her cable network? No problem. You'll get published. Have your own national radio show on NPR or KIIS FM? My marketing VP is going to love you. Built a blog readership that pulls in hundreds of thousands of people every month? OK, we can work with that.

Got none of the above (like most of the rest of the world)? Well, you're going to have a tough time getting published.

Over the past decade, the publishing industry has constricted; readership of traditional books has either gone flat or gone into decline. Thousands of bookstores nationwide have shut down, and the rise of the Internet has made it easy to steal entire works with the click of a mouse. (Hey, why spend $25 on a hardcover book when you can just copy the text off an obscure website?) All these factors and more have made it harder for traditional publishers to find the same kinds of success they used to take for granted. The result has been across-the-board cost cutting and only targeted promotion of perceived "higher profile" books. That means today's book marketing team faces shrinking or nonexistent budgets, tougher markets, and more pressure to perform.

In many marketers' minds, that situation has been translated to mean that the *author* must now bear the primary responsibility for promoting his or her book.

Is that expectation fair? Absolutely not. The author's responsibility *should* be solely to create a wonderful book that people will want to read (an extremely time-consuming job all by itself!). And besides, if you honestly have the ability to promote your book on OWN or some other widely known marketing channel, then you don't need a publisher. You can just self-publish, and let your pal O do the rest for you.

Ah, but publishing has never claimed to be a "fair" industry. It rewards only the strong, only those who can stay viable in the marketplace. So, even though it's not fair—and can occasionally be downright harmful for the industry—your book will often be rejected simply because the marketing VP doesn't see a legitimate way for you to do the marketing team's work on behalf of your book.

WHAT YOU CAN DO ABOUT IT...

1. Invest time in building an author platform.

This is hard for those who have dedicated themselves to a lot of the principles I outlined in the first section of this book. Why? Because instead of dedicating your time to honing your craft and creating works of art on a written page, you've now got to split your time between writing and platform-building. (Who knew a writer would be required to become a marketing professional?)

Still, we work within the situations we've been given, right? So the best way to build an author platform is to look for opportunities to combine your content writing with platform channels that are a natural expression of your work. For instance, if you write parenting books, you might try to place a parenting column in your local newspaper or in a national magazine. Then you can assume that the writing you do to reach the masses with your column will also be one day usable for a book that compiles those columns. But, of course, getting a newspaper or national magazine column is easier said than done.

At any rate, here are a few platform-building channels you can pursue in your spare time: high-traffic websites (try to become a content provider for some of these); high-traffic blogs; local newspapers; regional and national magazines; local, regional, and national radio programs; local, regional, and national television programs; political affiliations; national association publications; national speaking careers. Basically, any organization or publication that allows you to tell thousands and thousands of people about your new book will be welcome in the publishing board meeting, so look for opportunities to connect with those kinds of organizations/publications.

2. Network, network, network.

The more people you know, the more favors you can call in when your book releases. Hey, if you really do get into Oprah Winfrey's network of friends and/or colleagues, that makes a difference. If you meet Stephen King at a writer's conference and you two hit it off to the point of exchanging email addresses, that might turn into a high-profile endorsement for your next novel. Maybe a college student who's your Facebook friend will start interning for David Letterman. That connection could evolve into a guest spot on *The Late Show*—you never know.

So be someone who collects business cards, who stays in touch with entertainment industry colleagues, who stays in the good graces of people who know people. That kind of thing extends your platform and promotability, so make it a priority in your writing career.

3. Study DIY marketing and publicity strategies.

Last, but not least, remember that you don't have to be helpless when it comes to promoting your book. If you know how to reach eighty-five thousand people with your own press release, or how to take advantage of low-investment, high-exposure marketing channels, or even how to start a whisper campaign on the streets of New York City, that means something to a marketing VP. So hit your local library and carry home a stack of books on do-it-yourself marketing and publicity. Identify the strategies that seem feasible for you, and include a promise to implement them (along with the number of people you expect to reach) in your book proposal.

If you can market your book successfully through your own author platform, you become a valuable commodity to a marketing VP—and you get one step closer to getting that VP's vote during the publishing board meeting.

{ Reason № 34 }

You Don't Understand the Difference between Features and Benefits

Let's suppose you've got a great new book manuscript that features 365 all-new, fun activities for families. Do you know what my marketing VP is going to say about that?

"So what?"

And she's right to ask. So what? Why does your book matter to our readers? This is the "what's in it for me?" question every bookstore customer asks before swiping that debit card through the machine. That makes it the highest priority of any good marketing VP—and should also make it a high priority for you when you're creating the proposal for your book.

The big problem is that, while most authors know this is an important part of pitching a book, they don't understand the difference between "features" and "benefits." Don't let yourself be one of those ignorant (or lackadaisical) people! If you can master the art of benefit-speak, you'll make it very hard for any marketing VP to ignore you.

At its simplest, a book's "features" are anything it *has*. Its benefits are anything good it *does* for the reader.

re all kinds of nuances to that, and entire
tten on this topic by people who are much
for your purposes, if you can distinguish
k *has* and what it *does*, you'll be off to a
good start.

Here's a quick example of what I mean. Take that book we
mentioned earlier, the one with fun ideas for families. Here's
what it *has* (its primary "feature"): 365 fun activity ideas for families. And here's what it *does* (its "benefits"): 1) helps parents
and kids enjoy being together, 2) builds friendships between
siblings, 3) makes happy memories for kids…and so on.

You see the difference?

If not, don't be surprised when you receive my rejection
letter for your next book.

WHAT YOU CAN DO ABOUT IT…

1. Target identifiable benefits in one or more of the four basic categories.

OK, you should know that just about all benefits for a reader
typically fall in one of the four categories below. So, when creating your benefits summary, make sure to target one or more
of these areas:

- **Personal.** These are the things that promise to make a
  person feel better about himself or herself—promises of
  beauty, riches, spiritual growth, and so on. For instance,

"Reading this book will make you so pretty your poo will smell like sweet perfume!"

- **Social.** These are the things that bring social satisfaction or interpersonal success—promises of fame, better family relationships, improved dating relationships, or anything that generates a positive response from peers. For example, "Read this book and soon you'll be dating a woman who is so pretty her poo smells like perfume!"
- **Professional.** These are promises of success at work, career prestige, ability to fast-track up the corporate ladder, improved job performance, and so on. "Read this book and your boss will be working for you tomorrow!"
- **Noble.** These are promises to benefit "the greater good," or to bring moral and/or practical benefits for humankind or greater societies in general. "Reading this book will save the rainforest *and* cure cancer!"

2. Practice.

Sometimes it's easier to learn how to distinguish features from benefits with products that are *not* books. So take a look around your living room or kitchen and practice.

That blender on the counter…what are its features? (For instance, durable base, clear plastic pitcher, low-, medium-, and high-speed settings, and so on.)

Now, what are its benefits? (It can make me a super-yummy smoothie! It can help me with my mixing experiments! It can make it easy to spatter food chunks on my ceiling!) You get the idea.

3. Read a beginner's book about marketing copywriting.

The idea of features and benefits is the basic building block of any advertising copywriter's career, and as such it's almost always discussed in detail in any book about marketing copywriting. So if you still feel unsure about your ability to wow a marketing VP with benefit-speak, check out a book that deals with this topic in more depth.

There are plenty of these kinds of books to choose from (just search Amazon.com for "marketing copywriting"), but the one I've found the most helpful in my own career is Robert Bly's classic, *The Copywriter's Handbook.*

{ Reason № 35 }

You Have No PR-Worthy Accomplishments

On May 12, 2010, 712 people gathered in the gym at the 69th Regiment Armory in New York City to pelt each other with playground balls. As a result of this supersize contest, they set the Guinness World Record for "The Largest Dodgeball Game" in history.[25]

Were you there? And were you one of the last people standing when the Blue Team won the game?

If so, that's something I can use to jumpstart public relations efforts for you and your book—especially if your book is about sports, or dodgeball, or simply learning how to "seize the day." And my marketing VP is going to like hearing about the possibilities of that PR-worthy accomplishment.

You see, marketing VPs hate advertising. Sure, it's a necessary evil in their jobs, but it also costs a lot of money—and it doesn't often demonstrate a strong or measurable return on investment. Publicity, on the other hand, is free. It can deliver broad

---

25 "Fire When Ready," *ESPN* magazine (May 31, 2010): 22–23.

exposure similar to paid advertising, and since it's presented as part of editorial content, it often avoids the "commercial blindness" habits we consumers have developed toward advertising.

Look at it this way: At the time I am writing this, a half-page, four-color ad in a single issue of *Entertainment Weekly* magazine costs $104,305.[26] But a half-page review of your book right next to that ad costs…nothing. Which of those two options do you think is going to make my marketing VP's eyes light up?

Any significant edge you have in garnering publicity attention for your book is going to make a difference to my marketing team. And that's where your PR-worthy accomplishments come in. If I can tell my marketing team about your unique accomplishments as they relate to publicity opportunities for your book, it might be enough to tip the scales in your favor.

But what if you don't have any accomplishments worth trumpeting to the press? Well, that makes it harder to overcome the inherent skepticism my marketing team has about your book—and that could mean rejection.

WHAT YOU CAN DO ABOUT IT…

1. Make a list of your PR-worthy accomplishments as they relate to your book's promotion.

OK, honestly, you don't have to be a dodgeball champion to be PR-worthy. But it certainly helps if there's something about

---

26 *Entertainment Weekly 2010 Media Kit*, 4.

you or your book that would look good in a ne
line. So take time to make a list of things you think a
worthy about your book and about you. Some typical topics
that publicists hype when promoting a book are

- awards
- notable recognition (such as being named to a President's Council or being selected as keynote speaker at the National Happiness Day festivities)
- notable media exposure (such as being booked for *The Tonight Show* or featured in an article in *U.S.News and World Report*)
- unique milestones (such as winning a dodgeball championship)
- connection to notable events (such as being first on the scene after the 2010 earthquake in Haiti)
- anything that would spark interest if transformed into a two-minute spotlight on the local news

2. Highlight two or three PR-worthy ideas in your proposal.

Once you've identified your newsworthy angles as they relate to your book, go ahead and highlight them in your proposal. Suggest what can fairly be seen as "no-fail" angles that a publicist could use in the preparation of a press release about your book. Use bullet points and be sure to point out what kinds of audiences (magazines, newspapers, radio, etc.) would be likely to respond to those ideas.

3. Brush up on what a press release looks like and what it does.

Most writers are rightly focused on creating a book—not a PR plan. But if you want to win over a marketer, you're going to have to understand the way a marketer thinks about publicity. So take time to browse a website like PRWeb.com. Learn what goes into a press release. Read a few dozen and analyze them for strengths and weaknesses. Try your hand at writing a press release or two for your book and see how your PR compares to what the pros do.

Once you get into the publicity mind-set of the typical marketer, you'll be able to tailor your PR ideas toward the marketing VP—and beef up the appeal of your book proposal as a whole.

{ Reason № 36 }

You Are Not Able to Run a Grassroots Publicity Campaign for Yourself

In the movie *Bowfinger*, Heather Graham plays Daisy, a girl from Ohio who moves to California in order to make it in the movie business. When she steps off the bus in Hollywood, she looks around expectantly and asks no one in particular, "Where do I go to be an actress?"

Too many aspiring authors demonstrate Daisy's misguided optimism, thinking all they have to do is show up and a publisher will take care of the rest of the details required to make them a star. Unfortunately, in today's publishing climate the author is generally expected to contribute significantly to the star-making efforts for his or her book. This is especially the case with newer, or first-time, authors.

What that means is that every editor nowadays is asked by the marketing VP, "What's this author going to do to help us promote his or her book?" And your editor is going to expect you to answer that question with a clear, definitive plan.

Since most authors don't have easy access to a large public relations firm or the services of an independent marketing company on retainer, the best answer to that question is an opportunistic, grassroots publicity plan. If you can't provide that, my marketing VP is going to frown and start shaking his head.

From your perspective, this is an issue of both desire and skill. First, you have to *want* to promote your book on a grassroots level, exploiting your areas of influence and unique opportunities to get the word out about your book. Second, you must know *how* to do that effectively and affordably.

Remember the good old days when being a professional writer was only about, um, writing? Well, the good old days are gone. Now you are expected to be both a master of language who can write a phenomenal book and a savvy guerilla marketer who can start a grassroots firestorm of interest in said book.

It's not fair, but that's the way it is.

WHAT YOU CAN DO ABOUT IT...

1. Learn how to create a press kit.

OK, I'm not talking about a full-on, four-color notebook with pages of info and maybe a book-themed toy included (though I did very much enjoy a press kit once that came with Disney-themed cookies inside). You don't need that kind of overkill. And when you send your proposal, you don't even need to actually create a press kit—you just need to demonstrate that you *can*.

Most often nowadays, press materials are simply printed off a computer, folded in half, and stuffed inside the front cover of your book. So what you'll want to know is how to create that front-cover stuffing.

There's not enough room here to go into detail about each individual part of the press packet, but generally speaking, you'd want to include

- a press release announcing your book
- a pitch letter with specific story ideas related to your book (to send to media outlets when you request coverage)
- your bio
- suggested interview questions (these should be engaging, interesting, and something that would make it easy for you to be interviewed live)
- endorsements page (optional)
- your picture (optional)

2. Compile a personal database of local media and book retail outlets.

These are what would be considered "promotional outlets" or "media outlets." They are the places within your reach where your book might actually gain media coverage or gain a promotional event opportunity. For instance, local newspapers, regional magazines, local association newsletters and/or events, local bookstores (both national chains and independents), local grocery stores, regional radio stations, and so on.

Basically, anyplace that might tell others about your book should go into your database. Include contact names (such as the store manager, or editor of the lifestyle section of your newspaper) as well as full contact information for the outlet. If you can put together a database with fifty or more promotional outlet opportunities available in your grassroots network, that's something a marketing VP will be happy to hear.

3. Put together a formal publicity plan to include in your proposal.

Again, I'm not suggesting that you must create a formal press kit before you pitch your book to a publisher, but I am recommending that you tell an editor (so the editor can tell the marketing VP) about your unique plan for starting a grassroots effort on behalf of your book. One place you might want to visit to get help with ideas for grassroots PR ideas is the website PublicityHound.com.

Then, when you write your proposal, go ahead and include a section that talks about your future PR plans. Indicate that, in support of the book's release, you'll send a full press kit (tell what'll be in that kit) to your own mailing list of promotional outlets. If you can guarantee a book signing or two at your local Costco or Barnes & Noble bookstore, throw that in too.

List your plans in bullet-point format, and make sure you give the impression that you have both the desire *and* the skill to pull off a small-scale PR effort on behalf of your book. If you can, you've made the marketing VP's job easier—and that may be enough to make her take a chance on your new book.

{ Reason № 37 }

Amazon.com Reviewers Don't Like You

Here's a dirty little secret: Acquisition editors, agents, marketers, and salespeople all read Amazon.com reviews.

We do it to gauge if what you are telling us about yourself and your publishing history is accurate, or at least believable. We do it to see what supposedly impartial book buyers think about you and your writing. We check to see if you are engaging readers to the point where they feel they must talk about your work. And we do it to see if there's a general consensus among readers about your writing.

If an author sends me a proposal and mentions that he or she has previously published or self-published, I take a peek at Amazon. Consider it the publishing equivalent of Googling a blind date. I check first to see how many reviews your book has. If you've got ten or more reviews on a single book, that's more than the average, so I'm impressed. Next I check the star ratings on your books. I'm typically looking for how many people rated your book a 5, how many rated it a 4, and if anyone rated it a 1.

I'm hoping you've got mostly 4s and 5s in your star ratings, but I'll be honest, I also like it if you have a 1-star rating in there. I like to see if that 1-star hater is complaining about your writing skill (not good) or if that person simply disliked your opinions to the point that he or she was provoked to respond (actually a good thing, because it means your writing evokes emotion).

For instance, one of my authors once received a blistering critique of a suspense novel on Amazon.com. The reviewer admitted he'd been hooked by the story and read about halfway into the book before becoming offended that my author had mentioned God. And that was the basis of his 1 rating—he didn't like religious people and had been unhappy to discover my author was religious. My author was disappointed by the critique; I thought it was a great commentary on the effectiveness of her writing. The guy hates religious people…yet her writing was such that he read half her book anyway!

Now, what if your books are consistently getting 3 and 2 ratings on Amazon? Or if readers find your work cheesy or poorly written? Or worse yet, if your previous books aren't attracting any reviews? Well, that's a different story. That tells me people aren't terribly interested in your work, and my response is always the same: rejection by reason of Amazon .com reviews.

WHAT YOU CAN DO ABOUT IT...

1. Monitor your books on Amazon.com

Pay attention to what's going on in the reviews section of your books' listings on Amazon.com. If you're getting particularly good reader reviews on a book, don't be afraid to quote them in your next proposal. Or at the very least, point the acquisitions editor to them on Amazon and suggest that he or she share them with the marketing team.

This is especially important if you've self-published in order to get your writing career jump-started. A self-published book with no reviews, or with poor reviews, is death for traditional publishing opportunities. An unpopular self-published book is proof to me that, despite your intense desire to succeed, you just don't have what it takes to be successful in "real-world" publishing.

If, while monitoring your titles on Amazon, you discover that you're getting too many bad reviews, or very few reviews at all, then move on to suggestion #2 below.

2. Enlist your family, friends, and others to influence Amazon.com reviewer ratings.

The problem with Amazon.com reviews is that they are easily manipulated. All it takes is a dozen or so friends to tip the balance in your favor. Do editors and marketers know that? Sure we do. Are we going to contact each of the reviewers of your book to ask if they are your friends and family members? Not likely. So go ahead and take advantage of this flaw and use it to bolster your online reputation.

Enlist people you know (who also like you!) to post positive reviews on Amazon.com. Promise them a free copy of your book, or eternal gratitude, or whatever you think is best. Encourage friends to be honest, but not over the top in their reviews. For instance, hyperbole like "This is the best book since the Bible!" probably will be ignored. But if your friend is complimentary and identifies a few specific things that are highlights of your book, well, that looks good to a marketing decision-maker.

If you feel confident about the quality of your book, you might also contact some of the Amazon Top 100 Reviewers (accessible in the "People" section of the site) and ask permission to send them a copy of it. These are people who love books, and who've earned a reputation for reading lots of them, so often they'll be happy to get yours. If your book gets a positive review from a Top 100 Reviewer, that's also something worth mentioning to an editor in your next proposal. A word of warning though: If you're not absolutely confident of your content, *don't* send it to an Amazon Top 100 Reviewer. These folks aren't shy about posting negative reviews if they think a book deserves it.

3. Write great books that get great reviews on Amazon.com.

This is the best way to influence Amazon.com reviews— and by extension, influence the way a marketer or an editor will approach your next book. So, you know, you could just do this and let everything else take care of itself. I'm just sayin'.

{ Reason № 38 }

You Have No Internet Presence

O K, let's look at some of the numbers:

- There are 195 million *active* Internet users in the United States.[27]

- Americans rate the Internet as the number one "most essential" media source in their lives—ranking it higher than TV, radio, or newspapers.[28]

- An eye-popping 77 percent of Americans (nearly four out of five people) go online to buy books.[29]

- More Americans buy books online than at Target, Walmart, Sam's Club, BJ's, and Costco *combined*.[30]

---

27 The Center for Media Research, "Just the Facts..." *Research Brief* e-newsletter (January 6, 2010).

28 The Center for Media Research, "Digital Potpourri," *Research Brief* e-newsletter (April 23, 2010).

29 Zogby, *The Reading and Book Buying Habits of Americans*, a white paper commission by Random House (May 2008), 3.

30 Zogby, 3.

- The number one place *in the world* where Americans buy books: online.[31]

And you're telling me you don't have the time or interest to set up an Internet presence for yourself? Seriously?

Just last month I got a proposal from a college student telling me how she'd published her first book right out of high school and now she was ready for fame and glory with her second novel. I was curious, so I did what any guy does before a blind date.

I Googled her.

Nothing.

No author website, no blog profile, no Facebook page, no promos or reviews for her first book, no author interviews, no book excerpts, no chat room transcripts, nothing. The only thing I did find was that her first book was in the Amazon.com catalog—and (no surprise) it ranked an abysmal 2,481,729 in sales on that site.

The fact that she is anonymous online is killing this girl's chances at publication. My marketing VP already assumes that any new author is just another unknown who is unworthy of his support. How can I argue on this girl's behalf when a simple Google search confirms his dour presupposition about her? I just can't.

"Mike," you say to me, "there's too much online. It's too

---

31 Zogby, 3.

demanding—and too confusing. It moves so fast, don't have time to keep up. I just want to write books. Isn't that what's really important anyway?"

Look, you must understand something. My marketing VP doesn't give a flying fig about whether you're too busy or too old or too whatever to get yourself out there in the online world. All she cares about is that you are where book buyers are. And guess what? They're online.

Remember, once you decided to become a "professional" writer—someone who actually makes money from stringing words together—you also decided to pursue being a public figure. And if you're not able to be seen online? Well, you'd probably better stick to amateur status.

WHAT YOU CAN DO ABOUT IT...

1. Do the basics online.

At an absolute minimum, every aspiring author needs a website or blog profile page to showcase his or her ambition (more on this in Reason #40). This is both your billboard and your "Yellow Pages" ad on the Internet.

When you send me a book proposal, I expect to be able to find out everything I want to know about you simply by typing your name into a search engine. In fact, I may quote some of what I find out about you online to my marketing VP when we talk about your book. Do you really want someone else's random thoughts about you to dictate that conversation? Of course not.

So take charge of your online presence. Create a website or a blog profile that communicates everything great about you and your writing…and do it now.

2. Find a friend to handle your online presence.

If you really are too busy, or too intimidated, or "too old" to start up your own author presence on the Web, then you'd better find someone to do it for you. You can hire someone, but most often the best route is simply to find an Internet-savvy friend or family member and ask that person to set something up for you. With the abundance of online tools already out there, it's fairly easy to put up a bare-bones web page or blog profile, and anyone with regular Internet experience probably already knows what needs to be done.

So get help, and get a good author showcase for yourself out into the world of cyberspace…and do it now.

3. Grow up.

If you're still pouting about this online requirement for publishing success, stop it. This is the twenty-first century, and in this publishing climate, an Internet presence is mandatory for authors. So grow up and get yourself online…and do it now.

{ Reason № 39 }

Your Internet Presence Is Shoddy and Unprofessional

Now that I've badgered you into getting yourself online (see Reason #38), I do want you to know that there are dangers involved. If you treat your Internet presence as an afterthought or as something that can just be thrown together and subsequently forgotten, well, you take a pretty big risk.

You see, your presence on the Web is your claim to credibility. It's your business card. It's your customer promise. It's your product brochure. It's your company catalog, your product samples, your magazine advertisement, your author billboard—everything that makes you look attractive as an author. And it's accessible to *anyone*. If you allow your Internet presence to be poorly displayed, you'll make it easy for your book proposal to be rejected.

Look at it this way. Let's say you are hiring for an executive position at your company. You read two résumés and think they both look strong, so you invite both these candidates in for an interview.

The first candidate comes in dressed like she belongs in your company—professional, clean, stylish, and ready to interact with customers. She's energetic, attentive, and presents an intelligent, confident manner. The second candidate comes to the interview wearing a stained, ratty old T-shirt and sweatpants that say "Juicy" across the butt. She's obviously hungover, red-eyed, slack-jawed, and distracted, barely able to muster responses to the questions you ask.

Assuming the qualifications on their résumés are equal, which applicant are you going to hire?

That's the way I'm looking at your book proposal—comparing it to the other "applicants" for publication. When I and my marketing VP check you out online, you'll have a much better shot if we see an author who looks like the first candidate above instead of one who can't seem to get her "Juicy" sweatpants through the wash cycle.

WHAT YOU CAN DO ABOUT IT...

1. Guard your reputation online.

Remember, the Internet is forever. Anything you post online is accessible—even after you take it down (thanks to the wonders of caching).

This is great news if you are taking charge of your Internet presence, because you can pretty much dictate what people read or see about you online. If the majority of what's there is all praiseworthy and relevant, you're in great shape. No matter when or where I look online, I'm going to see a consistent message that communicates your credibility, authority, and publish-ability—something that reinforces a positive opinion of you in the marketing circles at my company.

Ah, but if you are lackadaisical about your Internet presence, or if you allow incomplete or incorrect information about yourself to languish happily online, then you're setting yourself up for failure. And the hard part is that you may not even know why you are failing. After all, my rejection letter to you isn't going to say, "Your web presence was weak, so we've opted not to publish your book." But that may indeed be the actual reason for rejection.

2. Don't ignore your Amazon.com AuthorCentral page.

If you've published *anything* at all, you've *got* to keep your author page on Amazon.com looking current and professional.

You see, every author listed in the Amazon.com catalog automatically has an author page created for them and kept on the site. If you ignore that page, Amazon enters just a few automatic entries—some books you published, a call for information, and a blanked-out photo indicating no current picture is available. This represents you poorly and should be corrected.

Once you register, you control things like which of your books are listed with your profile (and yes, Amazon often makes mistakes in this area), your author bio, your author photo, listings of your planned author events, promo videos, and even an author blog you can update regularly.

Why is this important? Well, 66 percent of online book buyers spend their book money at Amazon.com.[32] You do the math.

3. Point me toward your best side.

If you've taken care to manage your Internet presence, then don't take chances on my random search engine results. In your proposal, be sure to tell me I can discover more detailed information about you online. List your blog site, or the URL for your Amazon author page, or the address to your bio on your website. Then, my marketing VP and I will both go there first when we're checking you out online.

---

32 Zogby, *The Reading and Book Buying Habits of Americans*, a white paper commission by Random House (May 2008), 4.

{ Reason № 40 }

You Are Not Engaged/Poorly Engaged in Social Media

In 2008, barely one quarter of Americans aged twelve to adult were participating in social networking sites like Facebook or LinkedIn or MySpace. A scant two years later that number had *doubled* to 48 percent. What's more, among people ages twelve to thirty-four, more than two-thirds maintained a personal profile page on one or more of the social networking sites, and more than half (51 percent) of people ages thirty-five to forty-four did the same.[33]

What that means from a marketing perspective is sudden, direct access to millions and millions of Americans through their social network. What that means from the perspective of an aspiring author is that you have a stay-at-home method for broadening your author platform.

Of course this is a fine line to walk, as we all hate supposed Facebook "friends" whose only real purpose is to relentlessly promote whatever it is they're selling (cheap, handmade

---

[33] The Center for Media Research, "Digital Potpourri," *Research Brief* e-newsletter (April 23, 2010).

jewelry, anyone?). At the same time, if you can generate a decent following on a social network or two, that's going to make an impact when I'm discussing your marketing potential with my team.

In fact, one of the publishers I work with recently sent out a letter to *all* of their authors asking them to invest time and effort in cultivating their social network activity. Why? Because a strong social network presence can actually influence the exposure—and subsequently, the sales—of a book.

Which brings us to another interesting point on this topic. Because social networks have become such a marketing force in the book publishing industry, *we're all there*. In fact, in many places, a social network presence is actually part of the job description for an editor or marketing manager. Do you want to connect with editors? Find out what marketing team members value? Discover what publicists are promoting at present? You've got access. Just find us on Facebook or Twitter or LinkedIn or someplace like that. This world has never been more open than it is today, so go ahead and take advantage of that.

WHAT YOU CAN DO ABOUT IT...
1. Choose one of the "Big 3" and concentrate on building a following there.
OK, this is just my opinion at this point (no specific research to support this view), but my impression at present is that

there are three "big" players in the social network arena, and then a bunch of smaller ones. The three immediately recognizable social networks are Facebook.com, MySpace.com, and Twitter.com. All three have their strengths and weaknesses, so you'll want to check them all out before choosing where to focus your efforts.

Once you've picked your favorite of the "Big 3," then get busy populating your profile on that site, and work diligently to build up your following there. Because you could easily spend eight hours a day doing that, set yourself a manageable goal for social network investment. Some authors will commit thirty minutes each workday to that; others may want to dedicate only an hour a week. Find out what works best for you, and then stick to it. After a year or so, you should see significant results in your platform-building efforts.

2. Read up on social networking strategies.

Fortunately, although social networks are a recent innovation, they are no longer "new." That means you can hit your local library or your local bookstore and find several practical reference books to help you master the effective strategies for using these networks to your advantage. Here are a few that I'd recommend:

- *Social Networking Spaces: From Facebook to Twitter and Everything In Between* by Todd Kelsey

- *Social Media Marketing: An Hour a Day* by Dave Evans
- *The Facebook Era* by Clara Shih
- *Twitter Power 2.0* by Joel Comm
- *MySpace Marketing* by Sean Percival

3. Enjoy yourself.

Some people (like me) look at social network marketing as a chore. Other people (like my family members) see social networking as fun and a great way to keep connected with modern America. I will tell you from experience that you'll like this task much more if you allow yourself to view it from the perspective of leisure fun instead of a constant "to do" list.

So go ahead and enjoy yourself while you're building your social network platform. Take time to wander into interesting diversions, to smell the apps, so to speak. If you're going to do it anyway, you might as well find a way to like what you do, right?

{ Reason № 41 }

Your Title Stinks

If you bought this book off the shelf in your local bookstore, chances are good you followed this process when making your purchase decision:

1. You saw the words *77 Reasons Why Your Book Was Rejected (and how to be sure it won't happen again!)*, and that made you curious enough to read the back cover of the book.
2. You read the back cover, and that made you curious enough to check out the table of contents.
3. You skimmed the table of contents, and that made you curious enough to read part of the introduction.
4. You read part of the introduction, and that made you want to read the rest of the book.
5. Since you can't realistically read an entire book inside a bookstore, you decided to pay a few bucks and take the book home to read at your leisure.

Sounds pretty simple, right? It's actually a finely tuned

manipulation of your decision-making process, honed by decades of publishing trial and error. When we create the marketing materials for a book (such as title and subtitle, back cover copy, endorsement copy, and so on), we know the typical reader—whether buying in-store, online, or somewhere else—will almost always follow this sequence.

Guess what? If we fail to arouse a reader's interest in step 1 above—in the title package (title and subtitle)—we wipe out all our fantastic efforts in steps 2 through 5. Wasted.

Worse yet? We lose the sale.

Now, put on your marketing VP hat and re-read that list above. Do you see now the high importance of a superb title and subtitle combo for your book?

Yes, of course, 90 percent of the time the title you give your book in the proposal stage is going to change before it actually hits bookstore shelves. (With so much that depends on it, do you really think my marketing team is going to let a silly old author title a book without input from them?) But that's irrelevant in the initial publish/don't publish decision.

What is relevant is whether the title package you provided the editor is strong enough to make the marketing VP think, "Hey, this is something that'll get people curious enough to find out more…"

WHAT YOU CAN DO ABOUT IT...

1. Secretly title your book "Look Inside!"

When you boil it all down, every book title has only one purpose: to get the potential buyer to look inside.

If you can make that happen, and if what's inside (your content) is valuable to that reader, you will make a lot of money writing books. Think about it: More than half of the American book buying public (52 percent) admits that they "judge a book by its cover,"[34]—the centerpiece of which is that simple little title/subtitle combo. No wonder this matters so much to a marketing VP!

So, when making the working title and subtitle for your book, don't choose a boring sentence or phrase that merely explains what your book is about. Instead, focus on how your target reader benefits from your book, and ask, "What will make this person 'Look Inside'?"

2. Make a promise. Evoke emotion.

These are the basic elements of a compelling title for any book. Ignore them at your own risk (or at the risk that my marketing VP will ignore your book in return).

First, you've got to make a promise, either spoken or unspoken, to the reader. This is the great "benefit" that your book will give to anyone who reads it. (If you don't understand what

---

34 Zogby, *The Reading and Book Buying Habits of Americans*, a white paper commission by Random House (May 2008), 9.

that means, go back and re-read Reason #34.) For example, the promise of this book you hold in your hands is clearly given up front: You'll discover why editors reject books and how to make them stop rejecting yours. You see it, right?

Second, evoke a significant emotion in the reader. This is where you make the potential book buyer *want* your book. A suspense novelist, for instance, will want a title that evokes the thrill of being frightened (hence the term "thrillers"). A business writer will want a title that makes just the right amount of greed tingle inside a reader. And this book's title package (ideally) evoked an emotion of hope or enthusiasm in you.

If you can create titles that make a significant promise and evoke a desired emotion in readers, you are well on your way to winning over my marketing VP. So, you know, good for you!

3. Avoid confusion in a title, unless it's deliberate.
If you grab a bite to eat at the Saturn Café in Santa Cruz, California, and at some point need to visit the restroom, you'll be greeted by two doors. One door is labeled "Us." The other is labeled "Them." It'll be up to you to decide which of those doors leads to the men's room and which leads to the women's. That kind of ambiguous titling capitalizes on turning a reader's expectations into something unexpected. It's clever, deliberate, and attention-grabbing. A good thing.

Ah, but if you want to visit whorepresents.com on the Internet, it'll be up to you to decide whether that's a porn site called "Whore Presents" or a business database site called "Who Represents." That kind of ambiguous titling is accidental, confusing, and for many, reason enough to give up on the product. A bad thing.

So when it comes time to title your book, pay attention to potential misinterpretations and mistaken impressions. Take care to avoid anything that might confuse the reader or cause someone to misunderstand what your book is about.

son № 42 }

Your Introduction Is Useless

I 'm going to tell you two secrets now.

The first is an industry secret you should know so you can take advantage of it. The second is a personal secret I think will help illustrate the industry secret for you.

First, as a professional marketing copywriter, whenever I'm tasked with writing back cover or catalog copy for a book, I always ask for two things: the introduction and table of contents. Give me that, and I can make any back cover sing. In fact, we copywriters will often pull exact phrases from your introduction and use them in everything from back cover copy to catalog copy to press release copy and more.

The second secret is this: When I wrote the introduction to this book, I made sure to keep my future marketing VP in mind. In fact, after I had everything ready to show a publisher, I actually took significant portions of my introduction and adapted them into a mock-up of back cover text. I was hoping my editor would use that material to show his team how easy it would be to create marketing copy for this book—so easy, in fact, a good bit of their work had already been done for them.[35]

I knew that any marketing VP would view my writing through the lens of the requirements of his or her job. Since I wanted to enlist that person's approval, it fell to me to show I could give an introduction that would be minable for any and every copywriter who might be assigned to write the back copy of my book.

Ah, but what if my introduction had been boring? Or blathering? Or simply not benefit-oriented? What if my intro didn't clearly show the reader how he or she would gain from digging into the rest of this book?

The answer would be easy: rejection.

This actually applies to both fiction and nonfiction alike. In fact, sometimes in fiction a strong opening to your book is even more important. "I spend a lot of time trying to hook the reader in the first paragraph," says mega-bestselling author John Grisham, "even in the first sentence."[36]

One last example. Today I find myself forced to write a rejection letter to a new author I actually wanted to accept. I love her book concept. I like her credentials and the information she has to present. I even get a kick out of her title package.

But then I read her introduction.

---

35 Editor's Note: It worked.

36 As quoted in "Stewart Kills at Breakfast," *Publisher's Lunch Deluxe* e-newsletter, (May 27, 2010).

Despite all she has going for her, this author simply doesn't know how to craft an intro that draws the reader into the book to come. She views the introduction as a place to distribute facts instead of as an opportunity to create interest. Thus, there's nothing in here that a marketing copywriter can eventually use to promote her book. And that means a marketing VP is going to frown when (if) she reads it.

I know I could teach this author how to write a winning book introduction…but I just don't have the time. So today, against my own wishes, I'm going to reject her book.

Let's make that a lesson for us all.

WHAT YOU CAN DO ABOUT IT…
1. Give your introduction proper attention.

Some authors view an introduction as almost a "throwaway" element in their books. "Nobody reads those things, anyway," they tell me. "And besides, I want people to get into the meat of my book, not waste time in up-front materials."

That kind of viewpoint is both shortsighted and inadequate. The truth is, most potential buyers will judge whether to pay out for your book by what they find in the introduction. As such, this section deserves your deliberate attention. Never simply "throw together" an intro after you've written the later chapters in your book. And never rush through the intro on your way to writing the rest of the book.

A good rule of thumb is to write your introduction at least

twice: once before you write the rest of the bo
again after you've finished the manuscript. Doing
only helps your eventual reader but also helps your book
make the right impression on my marketing VP.

2. Understand that an introduction is different from any other chapter in your book.

Another mistake that newer authors make is assuming that an introduction is just another chapter in the larger book. Nothing could be further from the truth. For starters, in the typical book, the introduction shouldn't be longer than half the length of a normal chapter of the book. (There are exceptions to this rule—this book included!) Additionally, the introduction should function not so much as a funnel for information but as a map for relevant information as it relates to the book.

Most importantly, though, the primary purpose of your introduction should be this: *to create legitimate interest in the rest of the book.* Anything else can be deferred to later, if necessary. So when writing your introduction, make absolutely sure it captures the curiosity of your reader right up front.

3. Think like a copywriter.

You must remember that people like me are going to be mining your introduction for compelling phrases and descriptive markers to use in our advertising efforts for your book—including your book's back cover. If you give me tools I can use to market your book, you're going to get the attention of my marketing VP pretty quickly. After all, he's already looking for those little gems in your manuscript. If he finds them there, he'll quickly recognize that he's got a potential treasure in his hands.

So learn to think like a copywriter when working on your book's introduction. It's a different way of writing that requires a different way of thinking, but if you can master that talent, you'll greatly enhance your chances of success in the publishing business. See Robert Bly's excellent work, *The Copywriter's Handbook*, for more on this task.

{ Reason № 43 }

You Look Unprofessional

This reason for rejection is so mean.

After all, what difference should your looks make when we're deciding whether to publish a book? It's the inside that counts, not the cover, right?

Well, in a moral, human-centered way, of course that's right. But in a retail marketplace that really does judge a book by its cover, the way you look impacts your ability to be a public spokesperson for your book. And that matters to a marketing VP.

On the bright side, at least you're not gunning for a career in pop music. It's practically impossible to be unpretty and be a successful music artist—especially if you're a woman. It's not quite as extreme in the authorial world. You don't necessarily have to own a model-worthy appearance (well, unless you're writing diet/fitness books). But you do have to look clean, capable, and *professional*.

Remember, a marketing VP is always thinking about what will happen when your book is released. Will you come off well if her team gets you a TV interview? If you make a public appearance at Costco to do a book signing? If a magazine or newspaper interviews you and wants your picture to sit alongside their text?

In a book proposal, the most obvious way to present yourself as media-ready is with a professional, attractive press photo. Listen to the way PR expert Jacqueline Deval explains it:

> *For unknown authors, an interesting or unconventional author photo can help create a media profile, as newspapers and magazines are more likely to reproduce the image adjacent to a review or interview. Susan Minot's debut novel was promoted alongside her striking author photo. Sebastian Junger's first* book, The Perfect Storm, *was released along with images of the handsome author hoisting logs, presumably shot during his stint as a climber for a tree company. Dennis Lehane's publisher had him photographed to capture a moody noir image just like the atmosphere of his novels. Publishers view the image of the author as a vital part of the marketing campaign, particularly for novels and memoirs.*[37]

The sad truth of twenty-first-century America is that image

---

37 Jacqueline Deval, *Publicize Your Book!* (New York: Perigee, 2003, 2008), 54.

equals promotability in media. You can rail against it, or you can try to use it to your advantage.

WHAT YOU CAN DO ABOUT IT...

1. Cultivate a professional appearance.

If you send in a proposal without a press photo, or with a picture of you that obviously looks homemade, or that makes you look sloppy or unattractive or (worst of all) unprofessional, that's going to affect the perception of you by the marketing team. Again, that's not really fair, but that's the way things work.

So take care to cultivate a professional appearance in anything you send me. Notice I said "professional," not necessarily "beautiful." Of course, it doesn't hurt if you happen to be smokin' hot, but beauty isn't really the requirement here. What's required is that you look *professional*, like you belong on a TV panel of experts and authors; like you are comfortable with millions of people looking at you, judging your appearance.

If this is an area that doesn't come naturally for you, by all means get help. Enlist a local photographer or media-savvy friend to take a set of PR photos of you. Then pick the absolute best one and plaster it all over your book proposal, your website, and any other public place that requires your personal image.

2. Don't hate the player, hate the game.

On the surface, it's tempting to view the practice of using image as a factor in publishing with contempt, and to disdain all marketing VPs who hold that as a value in the publishing decision. You must remember, however, that marketing VPs are most often responding to a discriminating public's societal demands.

You know why image matters to marketing folks? Because it influences whether everyday readers like you and me demonstrate interest in the books they publish. If enough of us out here in the real world decided that only authors who didn't shower were most attractive and newsworthy, then that's what a marketing VP would demand.

But that's not the way it is, so you might as well make the best of a bad situation. When you hit the big time, you can use your star power to change this unrealistic expectation of authors.

3. Don't go the "glamour" route.

One big caution here: In recent years it's been popular for women to get "glamour" photos made. These are typically photo sessions where women get all dolled up with fancy makeup and flouncy clothes and assume model-like poses for a set of pretty pictures.

These little indulgences are fine for personal use—to share with a spouse, or friends and family. But they are *not* professional in the slightest, and they simply don't belong any-where in your proposal package. In fact, if you use a "glamour" photo as your press picture in your book proposal, chances are very good that I and my colleagues will laugh out loud while we reject your book unread. We're looking for people with a professional appearance…and this is not it.

{ Reason № 44 }

You Are a Poor Verbal and/or Informal Communicator

Let's start by calling this author Patrick.

I learned about Patrick during one of my acquisition editor stints. One of my fellow editors had enlisted Pat to team up with a more prominent author on a rush project—a book that was trying to capitalize on a currently popular trend and had to be completed quickly. According to my editor friend, Patrick's writing skill well exceeded that of his coauthor, so he ended up writing the bulk of the book. Lo and behold, their book became a national bestseller. Good news for all, right?

Except that during the media push for that bestselling book, Patrick and his coauthor appeared on TV together. The coauthor was polished, funny, and insightful in person. Patrick—who actually was the better expert on the topic, as well as the more articulate writer of the two—came off as stumbling and insecure. His skill with words on paper simply didn't translate into skill at verbal communication.

Here's the really bad news for Patrick: Both my marketing VP and my publisher saw his performance on TV. Based on that one interview, they came to the conclusion that Patrick simply wasn't a good verbal communicator.

About a year after his inspiring, bestselling success, Patrick returned to our publishing house with a new proposal. I thought it was excellent, and his editor also was a strong advocate for the book. But it was rejected in publishing board. Why? Both my marketing VP and my publisher simply couldn't get the image of Patrick's verbal communications failure on national TV out of their heads.

Did Pat deserve that rejection? Clearly not—after all, in spite of a poor TV performance, his book still had sold *several hundred thousand copies*. But that wasn't enough to change the perception of him in the eyes of my executives. In the end, they said the only way they'd publish something new from Patrick was if he were teamed up with the more articulate author from the last book.

That, friends, was a loss for author and publisher alike. But it happens sometimes, so you'd better be prepared for it.

WHAT YOU CAN DO ABOUT IT...

1. Never go unprepared into any kind of verbal exchange.

If an editor is seriously considering your work and preparing it for presentation at a publishing board meeting, he or she may call to talk to you personally about your book. *Never take that call until you feel completely ready for it.* Don't simply answer the phone when you see "ABC Publishing House" on your caller ID. Let it go to voicemail and listen to the message afterward.

If the editor is indeed asking to chat with you in person about your proposal, follow up with an email telling the editor you are enthusiastic about chatting, and asking if he or she can give you some idea of the specifics to talk about. Tell the editor you want to be sure to have all the information needed at the time of the call. Then set up a formal phone interview appointment, and knock 'em dead with your absolute preparation for anything that may be asked.

Listen, these kinds of calls are like a job interview. The editor is looking to get a sense of your personality and expertise. I've even had these kinds of calls where a marketing director listened in on the conversation. The thinking here is, if you can't talk professionally and passionately to an editor about your book, you'll self-destruct when (if) the marketing team puts you on display as a centerpiece in the future promotion of your book.

So follow the example of the Boy Scouts: Be prepared.

2. Plan to be the spokesperson for your own book.

If we can't trust you to be an effective spokesperson for your book, we can't trust that you'll be well received by the media and/or the public at large. That's why you must be more than a writer if you want to succeed in a publishing career. You must be someone who both understands and confidently participates in the requirement to be the physical representative of your book.

This means you should be prepared to handle public speaking, one-on-one interviews, panel talks, debates about your topic, and anything that may influence public perception of your book. Imagine it this way: Your book is president, and you are its press secretary. Can you comfortably handle the pressure that comes with that role? If not, my marketing VP is going to think twice before greenlighting anything with your name on it.

3. Get out of the house.

Many authors are introverts—this comes with the territory. After all, we spend hours a day all alone, tapping a keyboard or reading or lost in our own thoughts. That works fine from an editorial perspective. But since your book's success also depends on an extrovert's marketing perspective, you may need to build up your social skills.

So, you know, get out of the house every once in a while. Make time to hang out with friends. Talk to strangers at the airport. Attend your high school reunions. Go out for coffee with people from church. Grab a beer with folks from work. Get out of your comfort zone and into a social one at least once a week or so. If you practice being comfortable speaking in social situations, your comfort level in professional ones will improve as well.

{ Reason № 45 }

You Demonstrate No Knowledge/ Faulty Knowledge of Your Competition

Here's a tip: If you want to get an instant rejection letter from an editor, start your cover letter this way...

> *Dear Editor,*
>
> *I couldn't find any other book about [my topic here], so I decided to write one myself!*

Rejection.

Why? Well, there are several reasons—and any one of them merits your rejection letter.

First of all, what you've just shown is that you are willfully ignorant about publishing in general. In America alone, there are more than a million books published in a year[38]...and yet you can't find a single volume in all of history that somehow addresses a topic similar to yours?

That's just stupid—but writers do it all the time. Just today I got a query for a new book about the *Titanic*. Can

---

38 "New Book Titles and Editions, 2002–2009," BowkerInfo.com.

you believe it? The author actually said this to me: "There are virtually no current *Titanic* books available for adults." Funny, if you search for "Titanic" in the books section of Amazon.com, you'll discover *more than 2,000 books* on that topic. But this author thinks "there are virtually no current *Titanic* books" out there. That kind of ignorance just won't sell.

Second, you are willfully arrogant about your place in publishing. You claim to be the sole voice of authority on this particular topic—yet if that were truly the case, and if there truly were a demand in the market for that kind of expertise, then I'd be pounding on your door instead of you pounding on mine.

Third, you've shown that you are woefully unaware of the competition to your book—yet I can guarantee there will be other books competing with your book for available buying dollars. In fact, a quick subject search on Amazon. com will probably show me dozens of such books. (*Titanic* books, anyone?)

Fourth, I expect that your book should be somehow unique within publishing, but since you don't know what your competition is, you're woefully unprepared to tell me the truly unique qualities of your manuscript.

Fifth, if there really is no competition for your topic in the marketplace (as you claim), then there is no significant target audience that wants to buy a book like yours. Why should I invest my publishing house's capital in your book when there's no proof that people even want it?

Sixth…well, I could go on, but I think you're getting the point.

Competition in the marketplace is the foundation of our capitalist system. That means if you intend to be successful publishing within that system, you'd better have a clear, accurate understanding of the competition that's out there trying to take dollars away from your book.

I guarantee my marketing VP wants to know about that competition. If you can't give me that information because you don't know who your competition is, or because you have faulty knowledge of your competition, that tells me you don't know how to succeed in this business.

And that means I should reject your book.

WHAT YOU CAN DO ABOUT IT…

1. Use Amazon.com already.

In this age of unprecedented information access, I'm continually amazed by authors who tell me that they just can't find competitive books on a topic. I always want to ask, "What century are you living in?"

In Amazon.com alone you've got an instantly searchable database of almost every book currently in print, and for many books that are now out of print but still available in "used" or collectible format. What's more, for just about every book in the Amazon catalog, there is a summary of information that includes things like the publisher, the year published, retail pricing, and even a synopsis of the content.

All of those details, readily at your fingertips, tells you the what, when, who, why, and how of any book in their system.

And you're telling me you can't find that stuff anywhere? Please. Get off your butt and use Amazon.com already. You'll be amazed at what you'll find out about your competition there.

2. Become an expert on your marketplace.

Look, if you want to publish suspense novels, you probably don't need to worry too much about which parenting books are bestsellers right now. But you absolutely must know who people like Tess Gerritsen, Dean Koontz, Stieg Larsson, and Lee Child are. And you need to know why they dominate the suspense publishing category in bookstores.

So take time to become an expert in your chosen publishing category. Don't write your books in a vacuum—that only leads to stilted prose and, often, poorly developed duplication of other people's ideas. But if you know all there is to know about your competition, not only will that improve your writing, but it'll also improve your ability to conceive new ideas that are unique within the publishing landscape. My marketing VP will love that, by the way.

3. Don't be lazy.

If this is a temptation for you, re-read Editorial Reason #14 earlier in this book. The same principles apply when dealing with my marketing VP's demand for accurate knowledge of your book's competition.

{ Reason № 46 }

There's Too Much Competition for Your Book

I mentioned to you in Reason #45 that there are more than a million books published in a year. In fact, in 2009 there were 1,052,803 books published in America. Just under three-quarters of those (764,448) were self-published, while a little more than 25 percent (288,355) were released through a traditional publishing house.[39]

Do you understand what that means?

Today alone, traditional publishers will release, on average, 790 new books.

If you include books that were self-published (and you should because they also compete for dollars in the marketplace), that number jumps up to roughly 2,884 books released *every single day* in America.

At the same time, the largest percentage of Americans who buy books (50 percent) will purchase *fewer than one*

---

39 "New Book Titles and Editions, 2002–2009," BowkerInfo.com.

book per month (ten or fewer in an entire year).[40]

Is this starting to sink in for you a bit?

Let's be generous and say that the average reader will buy one book this month. There are *more than 87,000 brand-new ones* for that reader to choose from...plus the 87,000 that released last month...plus all the ones released all the months before today that are still vying for attention.

Now, put yourself in place of the marketing VP at my publishing house. How will you overcome all that competition to get the attention of a reader focused on a single book by a relatively unknown author?

That's the question that rings loud every time I bring your new proposal to my marketing VP's desk. To her credit, my VP is willing to tackle that huge chore, to find ways to creatively bring a new book to the front of a reader's mind.

Unless you send me a proposal on a topic that's already overdone in the marketplace. When that happens, those overwhelming numbers start to add up in her brain, causing her head to shake from left to right instead of nodding up and down.

You see, overexposure of certain themes often results in "topic fatigue" among buyers. (After all, when was the last time you bought a new book about The Atkins Diet?) And new books on tired-out topics don't often beat the

---

40 Zogby, *The Reading and Book Buying Habits of Americans*, a white paper commission by Random House (May 2008), 6.

odds—there's simply too much competition out there. If that's the kind of book you want to publish, chances are good you'll be rejected.

WHAT YOU CAN DO ABOUT IT...

1. Keep current on what's being published.

Hey, look at this as an excuse to hang out at your local bookstore. You like browsing the shelves anyway, don't you?

Seriously, at least once a month you should spend an hour or two just walking around Barnes & Noble or Books-a-Million or whichever is the favorite bookstore in your area. Check the shelves that carry books in your typical publishing categories, see what's new, what's old but still being carried in the bookstore, and anything else that looks interesting.

And yes, in case you're wondering, people on my side of the desk do that too. In fact, one of my former supervisors at a publishing house used to require that I spend time every month in a bookstore somewhere, checking out the competition. It was even a part of my annual job performance review. So are you surprised that your proposal is rated by the same measure?

2. Avoid overpublished themes.

This seems like obvious advice, and I wouldn't give it except that many authors don't understand it. If you see that everybody and their dog are publishing books that explain the basic principles of a flat tax system, well, maybe you don't need to add more of the same to bookstore shelves.

At the same time, don't assume that a popular theme is overpublished.

The key here is what you bring to the conversation. Do you have something new and unique to add to the flat tax discussion? Then by all means, go right ahead with your book. But make sure you really are offering something "new and unique." If you're not, you'll just get sidelined by topic fatigue and find your manuscript back on your desk with my rejection letter attached.

3. Make the competition irrelevant by becoming a pro at differentiating your book.

Ah, have I piqued your curiosity yet? If so, then read on to Reason #47, my young Padawan…

{ Reason № 47 }

You Aren't Able to Significantly Differentiate Your Book from the Competition

I learned this lesson the hard way early in my career, in my first year as an acquisitions editor for a midsize publishing house.

I brought to my publishing board what I thought was a very strong candidate for publication—a nonfiction book for teens. I'd done my homework. We'd had initial success publishing for the youth market recently, and this particular book was powered by strong writing and a credible author. I had good first-year projections from the sales team and unified support from editorial.

Time came for me to present, and things were going unexpectedly well. Voices of support were cropping up all around the table, and even my typically skeptical marketing VP seemed to be nodding his head in agreement. The only person who said nothing was my publisher.

Perhaps I took for granted that my publisher was already on my side. Or maybe I figured he wouldn't concern himself with marketing issues, since his real strength was in editorial. But I shouldn't have ignored his silence…

About four minutes into my pitch, I felt like this book was a shoo-in for approval. Then, while I was actually still speaking, my publisher stood up. He walked to a nearby bookcase and, in one swift motion, swept an armful of books off the shelf. Barely looking, he tossed them all onto the middle of the table, right in front of me. Then he did it again. And again. And he kept burying us in books until there were about two hundred of them spread out in lumpy stacks before us. Again without saying a word, he finally walked back to his chair and sat down.

Then he looked me straight in the eye and said, "Your book is no different from any of these."

And that was it.

Discussion over.

Decision made.

We didn't even bother to vote on the proposal I was advocating. I'd been unable to compellingly differentiate the book I was pitching from the hundreds of books on our table—let alone the hundreds of thousands in the marketplace at large. I should have easily predicted the final decision:

Rejected.

WHAT YOU CAN DO ABOUT IT...
1. Don't get caught unprepared when the books start flying.

Being able to significantly differentiate your book from the competition is simply a nonnegotiable for just about any publisher. In your proposal, this should fall under a section called "Competitive Analysis" or "Market Analysis."

Typically what this includes is a list of three to five prominent books that are currently popular in your selected category. (For instance, if you're publishing in the cookbook category, then you'd probably include titles by people like Paula Deen, Jillian Michaels, Anthony Bourdain, and maybe even Julia Child.)

For each of these potential competitors, you'd then include a short summary of content (I usually just copy this, with credit, straight from Amazon.com). Then you'd show two things. First, how your book compares favorably to the popular one. (For example, "Like Paula Deen's work, my cookbook has classic homestyle recipes with immediate appeal to middle-class families!"). Second, you'd show how your book differentiates itself in a unique way to attract buyers to yours. ("Unlike Deen's book, my cookbook delivers remarkably tasty recipes without overindulging in high-risk health habits for family members, like excess butter and fat.")

It's a balancing act, true. You have to show that your book has a similar audience appeal like the popular one, and yet you also have to show that your book is *better*. It takes practice, but it'll pay off if someone on the publishing board likes to throw a few books around the table.

2. Take a lesson from Grand Central Station.

On a chilly Saturday in 2007, Grand Central Station came to a standstill. That's when about two hundred "agents" from Improv Everywhere showed up on the Main Platform and simply froze in place. The result was a dramatic, attention-grabbing spectacle—and one of the best visual examples of the power of differentiation that I've ever seen.

No, these "agents" didn't loiter around reading books. But they did enter a "crowded marketplace" and, in only seconds, made themselves clearly stand out from the competition (the thousands of others in the station) in such a way that everybody took notice.

So here's what I'm suggesting: First, watch the online video "Frozen Grand Central" (available at: http://www.youtube .com/watch?v=jwMj3PJDxuo). Then ask yourself these questions: Why did just standing still make thousands of people stop and take notice? What principles about effective differentiation do I see at work in this situation? How can I apply those principles when differentiating my book from its competition?

If you can answer those questions well, my marketing VP will notice your book...even in Grand Central Station.

3. Don't overdo it.

While I can't emphasize enough the absolute necessity of being able to effectively differentiate your book from the competition, I do want to warn you that there are risks to going too far with this. Remember, the goal here is to show that your book delivers some unique benefit others don't have—not to give an exhaustive list of every book published on a similar subject.

I remember one time looking at a book that I thought had potential—until I saw the market analysis. The author had certainly done his homework. He'd listed close to twenty other books on the topic, most of which I'd never heard of. All that did was convince me that his subject was currently overpublished and unable to sustain a new entry in that category, so I rejected on that basis.

So be careful to stack the comparisons in your favor. Stick with three to five competitors, and you should be fine.

You Can't Quickly Evoke the Right Emotions When Talking about Your Book

For sale: baby shoes, never worn."[41]

Only six words, but they evoke the gamut of emotion in the reader: curiosity, tenderness, joy, and sorrow.

In fact, this is a complete short story written by Ernest Hemingway, and one that he called his best work. Well, with that kind of skill, Papa Bear must have made his marketing VP proud indeed.

Now, you don't have to be a legendary writer of fiction in order to succeed with your latest pitch to a publisher—but you should be able to quickly, succinctly evoke the desired emotions when talking about your book. This will happen primarily in the content summary section at the beginning of your proposal. And, unlike Hemingway, you have much more than six words to use! But you'd better be able to do this quickly, most likely in fifty to sixty words (or less).

---

41 Ernest Hemingway, as quoted in Wired.com, "Very Short Stories."

Why is it so important to be able to evoke emotion in a silly little summary paragraph? Because emotion dictates decision-making. Neuroscientist Benedetto de Martino is just one of many researchers to confirm this connection. After his lengthy experiment on decision-making among gamblers, he reported, "We found that everyone showed emotional biases; no one was totally free of them."[42] In *How We Decide*, Jonah Lehrer chronicles medical studies on patients with damaged emotion centers in the brain to arrive at the conclusion that "emotions are a crucial part of the decision-making process…a brain that can't feel can't make up its mind."[43]

So, in the content summary at the beginning of your proposal, you've got about sixty words to make the brains of your editor, marketing VP, and sales VP *feel* the right emotions that will prompt them to buy your book. Use those words wisely, and you've just increased your chances of actually making it to the next publishing board meeting.

WHAT YOU CAN DO ABOUT IT…
1. Take charge of your reader's emotions.
Of course, in the case of your content summary, your readers are the editor, marketing VP, and sales VP—but since you know who they are, that gives you more power than you likely

---

42 Quoted in Jonah Lehrer, *How We Decide* (New York: Houghton Mifflin Harcourt, 2009), 106–107.

43 Lehrer, 15.

have used in the past. When composing your content summary, read past the words and into the emotions those words evoke. Take charge of what your reader will feel when he or she first encounters the quick description of your book.

For instance, are you selling a book about solutions to dolphin de-population in the Pacific Ocean? Then you'll probably want to open with a statement that evokes concern in the reader. ("When all the dolphins are gone, humanity will be next in line.") Then you'll want to move into a statement that brings relief and/or optimism. ("But that's not going to happen while you're around.") And you'll close with a line that sparks enthusiasm and/or heroic impulses in your reader—and that maximizes your book's importance in those feelings. ("This book will show you how to save the dolphins…and save your world.")

2. Be careful not to unintentionally evoke the wrong emotion.

We live in a politically correct world, and that means paying attention to potentially offensive terminology (unless, of course, your intent is to offend). Regardless of how you feel personally about political correctness, it makes no sense to offend when you don't have to do so.

If you open your summary by casually referring to the Holocaust as myth, for instance, you've immediately irritated a majority of your readers. If you use a word like "niggardly"—even though this word refers to being miserly and has nothing to do with a common racial epithet—many will still feel anti-racist sentiment toward you and your work as a result.

So, as you're writing to evoke desired emotion, be careful that your words don't unintentionally evoke the wrong emotion.

3. Pay attention to how you feel.

Try this creative exercise for writers. First, list seven motivating emotions, such as anger, curiosity, excitement, and so on. Then assign each emotion to one day of the week.

Take a notepad with you as you go through your week, and every time you feel that day's assigned emotion, jot down the circumstances or catalyst that prompted that emotion to surface in you. This could be something as simple as watching a Kodak commercial or being cut off in traffic.

At the end of the week, review your journal entries and ask yourself, "What principles can I learn about evoking emotion from these experiences? And how can I use those principles to evoke emotion when I'm talking about my book?"

{ Reason № 49 }

You Can't Provide Impactful Endorsements for Your Work

All right, first I'm going to tell you the reality behind endorsements, then I'll tell you why that reality is irrelevant.

You might not know this, but endorsements on the back of a book are nothing more than people doing favors for each other. They rarely reflect actual praise for a book. In fact, most times, the people who wrote the endorsements didn't even read the book. (Of course, that's not true of the endorsements on the back of *this* book...wink wink, nudge nudge.)

Here's the way it works. I do a friend a favor—say, endorse her book or help him find an agent, or introduce her to my editor. She's subsequently a hit in the marketplace (yay for her!). So when my next book rolls around, I politely ask her to do me the small favor of endorsing my book.

Well, she knows two things: 1) She may want a return favor from me in the future (say, a foreword for her next book), and 2) if she puts her name on the back of my book, that means all my readers will see her in a positive light...which could create add-on sales next time she publishes. So she graciously writes a sentence or two saying how wonderful my book is, and we both go on with our lives.

This is why it's so important to network in the publishing industry, to make friends, and to stay friends with people of influence and/or people who might become people of influence. And that's why the reality is that most (not all, of course) blurbs showering praise on a book and plastered all over the back cover are really just a you-scratch-my-back-and-I'll-scratch-yours sham.

Now, here's why that reality is irrelevant: because endorsements impact sales.

Believe it or not, more than one-third of American readers say they "buy a book because of a quote from another author."[44] Crazy, huh? But true. Plus, stellar endorsements give a marketing team another hook to use when shouting about your book to the media—and they create PR goodwill from people who view the endorser favorably.

In fact, I've even had a book denied in publishing board simply because I couldn't promise one specific person would endorse that specific book. Again, crazy, huh? But that's the way it works sometimes.

So, when you're preparing the proposal for your next book, be sure to include a section that highlights people to whom

---

44 Zogby, *The Reading and Book Buying Habits of Americans*, a white paper commission by Random House (May 2008), 9.

you are somehow connected and who, when asked, are likely to endorse your book. If the names on that list are recognizable, you'll definitely get my marketing VP's attention.

WHAT YOU CAN DO ABOUT IT...

1. Stay networked.

This is the key to securing solid endorsements for any book. Like most things in life, it's not what you know but whom you know. So be someone who knows a lot of people.

When you attend a writer's conference, be the person who meets people. In some cases, go ahead and schedule appointments even though you don't plan to pitch anything to a certain agent or editor. Tell them that you just wanted to meet them, get their advice on the industry, and let them know you exist in case you send them a pitch sometime in the future.

Join online writer's groups, write reviews of books by authors you like, post comments on author blogs and websites. Just stay in the game, so to speak, even if you don't yet have a play to call. Next time you need a great endorsement, that networking may just pay off.

2. Don't assume only authors can be endorsers.

My wife once published a book called *The Low-Fat Lifestyle*. (Great book by the way—sincerely!) If you look at the back cover on that book you'll see an obligatory endorsement from a prominent women's author/editor. Above that one, however, you'll see an endorsement from a guy who's never written a thing in his life.

So why does he rate as a significant endorser for this book? He's a medical doctor, an accomplished physician, and an expert in the field of health and medicine. That makes him a person who immediately lends credibility to the healthy ideas my wife included in her book.

So don't assume your endorsers must always be other writers. Find credible experts in the field who can lend their authority to the material covered in your book. Sometimes that carries more weight than even a bestselling author.

3. Stay on good terms with your editors.

John Maxwell is a *New York Times* bestselling author, one of the nation's foremost experts on leadership, and a well-respected business guru to millions. I personally have never met, nor spoken to, nor even exchanged emails with Dr. Maxwell. Yet he wrote an entire foreword to one of my books.

How did I pull this off? Well, I stayed on good terms with an industry friend who went on to become both my editor and Dr. Maxwell's editor. When the time came for collecting the foreword and endorsements, this editor did me a huge favor and contacted John Maxwell on my behalf. (And hey, if you're reading this, I still owe you one, Mark!)

Like I said, it's not always what you know, but whom you

know. So stay on good terms with your editors—even through all the waves of rejections. Those people may one day do you a big favor when it comes time for endorsements.

{ Reason № 50 }

My Marketing Team Tried to Promote a Similar Book in the Past, and It Failed

One of the hard facts of life is that past experience influences present expectations. That means you are often judged by the performance of people who came before you, regardless of whether that judgment is fair.

Robert Cialdini, professor of psychology and marketing at Arizona State University, explains it this way:

> *If you are asked to pick up a ten-pound weight in a gymnasium, it will appear lighter if you had first picked up a twenty-pound weight and heavier if you had first picked up a five-pound weight. Nothing has actually changed about the ten-pound weight—except your perception of it. This psychological process is not limited to weight; it holds for almost any type of judgment you could make. In every case the perceptual process is the same: Prior experience colors perception.[45]*

---

45 Robert B. Cialdini, Noah J. Goldstein, and Steve J. Martin, *Yes!* (New York: Free Press, 2008), 167.

Few things color a marketing VP's perception more than failure. In the high-pressure world of publishing, every perceived failure in promoting a book carries with it the threat of a lucrative marketing career cut short. Someone still smarting from that kind of recent failure is unlikely to do anything that might bring the same results again.

So, if you come to my publishing house with your great new idea about the joys of deep sea fishing, my marketing VP is immediately going to think about all the wasted time, money, and effort his team spent on last year's book about fly fishing. And he's going to start shaking his head at the mere thought of possibly going through that again.

"We tried that before," he'll tell me. "Didn't work. What else you got?"

No, it's not entirely fair. But the rejection letter you get is the same anyway.

WHAT YOU CAN DO ABOUT IT...

1. Justify your target audience.

Following the suggestions included back at Reason #6 will help you with this, but the main idea here is to target an audience that is both clearly identifiable and of significant size to support a book's publication. Then show how and why that audience will absolutely want your book—even if they didn't want a similar book in the past.

If you can use demographic statistics here—for instance,

the number of deep sea fishermen and women in the United States or the annual sales figures of the deep sea fishing industry as a whole—that certainly helps my marketing VP reframe his experience in terms of your potential. Add on ways you intend to help your publisher reach that audience—say through speaking at the National Deep Sea Fishing convention, or by writing a column in *Deep Sea Fishing Monthly* magazine, or whatever—and you just might make my VP forget there ever was a fishing book before yours came along.

2. Differentiate. Differentiate. Differentiate.

Remember, you've got to be able to show that your book is uniquely positioned for success in the marketplace anyway. If you do a good job of that up front, then it could be irrelevant that my marketing team failed on a previous book because your book is so much more prepared to make an impact in the market.

If you still feel fuzzy on this, go back and re-read Reasons #45, 46, and 47 until you could teach a seminar on that topic alone. Trust me, it's that important.

3. Find a company that's more successful in the areas you want to sell.

In the big picture, a publisher that has trouble selling books similar to yours may not be the best place for you to land anyway. After all, an attitude of failure toward a certain topic or category of books can often become a self-fulfilling prophecy.

"We've never been successful with these kinds of books in the past, so why try to be successful with this book in the future?"

A marketing VP who turns down your book because of past failures with a similar one may actually be doing you a favor. That VP is giving your book an opportunity to succeed with a different publisher who is better in that area.

So if you find yourself getting rejected because of someone else's bad experience in the past, take it as a gift instead of a curse. Do a little more homework and find a company that's better equipped to contribute to your book's success. It may all work out for the best in the end.

{ Reason № 51 }

My Marketing VP Is Unfairly Prejudiced Against You

Let's see…for this one we'll call our hero Andy.

Andy is a novelist I've worked with on several occasions. He's an outstanding writer of fiction, a hard worker, and just a great guy to boot. When I worked for a while acquiring suspense fiction, I lured him away from a competing publisher and locked him up with a three-book contract. His first book out of the gate hit our industry bestseller list. Happy days.

A few years later I joined a different publishing company, and one of the guys on the sales and marketing team had come from that competing publisher where I'd stolen Andy away.

Well, for me, bringing Andy to my new publishing house was a no-brainer. So he worked up a proposal for me, I prepared it for presentation at publishing board, and away we went.

Except for that other guy. For some reason (I still haven't figured out exactly what it was), when he saw Andy's name on the agenda, he immediately started badmouthing my author to anyone who would listen—especially to my marketing VP.

"We could never sell Andy's books at my old publisher," he said.

"And yet you published more than a dozen of them," I said.

"We could never get people to notice him in the market-place," he said.

"And yet every person here knows who Andy is," I said.

"I'd never publish Andy," he said.

"I did publish Andy," I said, "and he hit the bestseller list."

It was surreal, and awkward, how determined this guy was to sabotage Andy's new book. And he almost won. In the end, the marketing VP appeared convinced by this one negative guy, but the sales VP and publisher overruled him and voted to publish.

Still, if Andy hadn't had verifiable market success already, that kind of unfair prejudice against him would have derailed his chances with my company. And people in publishing board can be prejudiced against an author for all kinds of strange reasons—because of a topic, because of a genre, because of a friend of a friend who didn't like a book, or whatever.

Hey, if it can happen to Andy, it can happen to you.

WHAT YOU CAN DO ABOUT IT...

1. If you can help it, don't piss anybody off.

Yes, I know, sometimes you can't help it. Especially in this industry where so many people are egotistical jerks. So I'm not saying you should never make anybody mad at you (hey,

I'm fairly certain there are people out there who grimace when my name is mentioned). But I am saying that, if you can avoid it, don't provoke an industry colleague into a fight. Don't call people names. Don't demand satisfaction or chew someone out because they dunya wrong.

That kind of stuff always comes back, and sometimes it'll return to you in ways you can't even see (like in a closed-door publishing board meeting) but which have significant impact on your publishing career.

So the age-old advice of the golden rule still applies: do unto others as you'd have them do unto you.

2. Increase your odds.

This goes back to market research and knowing who is publishing the kinds of books you want to publish. If you've only got three legitimate companies as your target publishers for a book, and you've already managed to piss off somebody important at one of them, that knocks out one-third of your opportunities just because of a personality conflict.

On the other hand, if you've got ten potential publishing partners, and one of them is unfairly prejudiced against you, that still leaves 90 percent of your options open. So go ahead and play the odds a bit, and make sure you target a good number of editors with your next proposal.

3. Let your talent do the talking.

I once had a fantastic proposal from a successful romance author who wanted to branch out into romantic suspense. The president of my company wouldn't let me publish it.

"She's a romance author," he said. "She can't write suspense."

But did I mention it was a fantastic proposal?

This author didn't waste time complaining to me about how unfair we were being toward her and her chosen genre. Instead, she took that book to a different company. They recognized the potential that I did—and then some. Today she's one of the most reliable romantic suspense authors out there. In fact, you've probably seen her hogging up shelf space at Walmart and quite likely have read one of her books (if you like romantic suspense).

In the end, she let her talent do the talking, and that was more than enough.

{ Reason № 52 }

My Marketing VP Doesn't Care about Your Topic—and Doesn't Think Anyone Else Will Either

Elizabeth Gilbert has made gobs of money—and generated a huge amount of media coverage—with her memoirs *Eat, Pray, Love* and *Committed*. That means your memoir of transformative living should have equal appeal to a publisher, right?

Wrong.

Because, despite the documented, exceptional success of people like Gilbert or James Frey (root canal, anyone?) or Julie Powell, memoirs remain a category of low reader interest overall. In fact, according to one prominent study, 99 percent of readers out there couldn't give a flying fig about those books. That's right, only 1 percent rated memoirs as a "favorite."[46]

How about a biography of Nat King Cole then? Legendary singer, extraordinary life. People will eat that up, right?

---

46 Zogby, *The Reading and Book Buying Habits of Americans*, a white paper commission by Random House (May 2008), 11.

Well…it could happen. But it's not likely. According to that same poll, only 5 percent of readers favor biographical topics.[47]

Here's what my marketing VP knows about publishing: Subject matter matters. In significant numbers, readers report that a book's subject is what "first draws" them to a book, and also the "most important factor" in their most recent book purchases.[48]

That means, if my marketing team wants to get public attention for a book—in magazines or newspapers, on the Internet or TV or anyplace buzz can build for a book—they've got to be sure that book's topic is compelling. Hey, my marketing VP isn't stupid. It took a lot of schooling and real-world experience for her to get where she is today. So before she'll give a thumbs-up on your newest book proposal, she's going to ask herself, "Do I care about what this book's about? Does anyone?"

Chances are good that my marketing VP is going with her gut on this one. If your book's topic doesn't make her care, she'll assume no one in the real world will care either. And that means your book never gets a chance.

---

47 Zogby, 11.

48 Zogby, 11.

WHAT YOU CAN DO ABOUT IT...

1. Do the obvious: write about something that lots of people care about.

What do you care about? Make a list of your top ten.

If you're like most people, these are probably on your list: Family. Health. Love. God/Religion. Work/Career. Why do I know this? Because those are basic needs and interests of just about anyone. If you write a book on one of those topics, chances are good that people will care about it—especially if you can make sure your approach to the topic is unique and different and relevant to your target reader.

Does that mean you can't write about anything else? Of course not. But it does mean that, no matter what topic you choose, it's up to you to make sure it somehow relates to something that lots of people care about. Is there a way to write about the social habits of fire ants and somehow make that appeal to your reader's need for family connections? Probably, if you're any good as a writer, that is. How about a novel centered on commerce in the ancient Egyptian world? If you can bring out themes of love and work in your story, sure, people will care about that.

The real question is whether you're paying attention to the themes in your book. If you are, then you should be able to write something that my marketing VP will care about.

2. Highlight themes in your work that are similar to themes my marketing team has succeeded with previously.

Again, this isn't a suggestion for you to copycat someone else's work. But it is a little advice to help you point yourself in the right direction when it comes to choosing topics for your books.

Look at a publisher's website, or on bestseller lists, or in the pages of your favorite glossy magazine. See which books are getting lots of attention from media outlets—those are the ones giving marketing people success. These books could be any genre or any category—nonfiction, historical, fantasy, western, even memoir. Identify the core themes that these books are about, and then pair them up with the responsible publishing house.

When you next pitch to a publishing house, see what themes you paired up with them. Then highlight how those topics show up in your book as well.

3. Memorize this principle: "Subject matter matters."

Then, when you're choosing what to write about next, make that decision with more than just you in mind. Ask yourself, "What do I like that millions of other people also like? And what can I say to them on that subject?"

If you're careful to make your subject matter matter, the odds are pretty good my marketing VP will care whether your book becomes part of my future publishing list.

Bottom Line—You Weren't Good to Mama

In the hit movie musical, *Chicago*, Queen Latifah plays Matron Mama Morton, a media-savvy, happily dishonest warden at a women's prison. As a way of welcoming new inmate Roxie Hart (Renee Zellweger) into her world, Mama sings a little melody that gives the basic rules for success within the walls of her prison. What it all boils down to is this:

"When you're good to Mama, Mama's good to you."

Why is that important for you to know? Because in the world of publishing, the role of Matron Mama Morton is played by my marketing VP. (Well, except for that "happily dishonest" part.) That person holds the keys that can set your book free from its unpublished prison and send it on to its rightful renown. The problem is that we authors most typically aren't good to Mama. In fact, we view Mama with contempt, or irritation, or worse.

For instance, when a book fails after publication, authors will almost always point a finger at the marketing department. "My book just wasn't marketed the way it should have been," we'll shrug and say. "It never had a chance." By the same token, when a book succeeds, we authors generously ignore the marketing team and soak up the credit for ourselves, assuming it was our writing skill and passion that was rewarded by an adoring marketplace.

The truth is, professional success as an author depends equally on your ability to write *and* your ability to market your work. Ask just about any self-published writer. It takes much more than mere talent with words to make an impact with the book-buying public. It takes a proactive, productive partnership between editorial and marketing to be the driving force behind any significant sales success.

And marketers know that. What's more, my marketing team is sick of being blamed (by you, by the sales department, by your editor) for failures—past, present, and future. They want to contribute to, and be credited for, making a book a successful publication.

And so the bottom line is this: If you can make yourself a valuable contributor to my marketing VP's success, you will be successful yourself. You'll have transformed that generally negative person into one of your biggest allies in the decision-making process.

Remember that the next time you want to publish a book. Be good to Mama, and she'll be good to you.

WHAT YOU CAN DO ABOUT IT...

1. Make yourself indispensable to my marketing VP.

Marketing guru and mega-bestselling author Seth Godin says, "If you're not indispensible (yet), it's because you haven't made that choice."[49]

Mr. Godin is right. If you're not yet indispensible to the marketing VP at my publishing house, it's because you've chosen not to be. Over the last few dozen reasons for rejection in this book, I've given you a quick glimpse at what my VP needs to get his marketing team excited about making your book successful. I've shown you, pretty clearly, how to make that VP think you're indispensible to his own personal success.

Trouble is, most authors want to skip over the marketing requirements for publishing success. "That's someone else's job," we tend to think—and sometimes even say out loud. Still, writers who are in the early stages of their careers simply don't have the luxury of that kind of attitude.

So choose to make yourself indispensable to my marketing team. No, it's not easy. But if you do that, you'll find you have a productive future in publishing after all.

2. See yourself as an ally of the marketing team.

This is simply an attitude change on your part.

Look, my marketing VP is already biased against you. She's going to shine a spotlight on all your weaknesses and argue

---

49   Seth Godin, *Linchpin* (New York: Portfolio, 2010), vii.

against taking any real risks with an unproven author.

So what? Either you can fight that criticism and take whatever lumps might come in the process. Or you can picture yourself on the marketer's team and make yourself an ally of my VP by creating something she actually wants. Guess what? When you do that, she'll shine her spotlight on all your strengths and become a vocal advocate of you and your book to all the other members of my publishing board.

And believe me, having a marketing VP as an ally goes a long way toward publishing success, both before and after your book is contracted.

3. Be good to Mama.

Before you send anything to an editor, ask yourself, "What's this editor's marketing VP going to ask about this proposal?" Seriously, go ahead and make a list of anticipated questions that will concern the marketing team about your book.

Next, figure out how to answer all those questions in ways that are "good to Mama"—that is, in ways that show the marketing VP you're doing the best you can to make the marketing team's job both easier and more successful.

This may take some thought on your part, and some questions may strike you as impossible to answer. But if you can think of the questions, you can bet your editor's marketing VP is going to ask them. So tackle them head on, and be that rare author who actually makes Mama happy with a new book proposal.

$\left\{\text{ Part Three }\right\}$

Sales Reasons for Rejection

You Are Not a Celebrity

Wow, this reason for rejection is so unfair.

And it's not even legitimate, really. Lots of celebrities write books that never crack a bestseller list and shouldn't have been published to begin with.

Nonetheless, I have on several occasions sat in a room with a group of salespeople and asked the question, "What kind of book would you most like to have to sell to bookstores next season?" One of the first answers has *always* been, "Can you get us a book by a celebrity?" They don't even care who the celebrity is, just that the author is one.

Why do salespeople want books by celebrities? It's actually a *brand/buy* issue. If I give them a book by, say, Jay Leno, the brand for the book is already established and successful in the marketplace. When they start contacting book buyers for Barnes & Noble or Walmart, my sales team doesn't have to spend a lot of time explaining and cajoling those people to stock the book in their stores. The book buyers already know who Jay Leno is; they know their customers know; and they know many people will go ahead and *brand/buy* the Leno book sight unseen—that is, they'll *buy* it simply because they're already sold on the "Jay Leno" *brand* name from late night TV.

So what if you're not a celebrity with a built-in brand name that can guarantee a certain amount of sales simply because of your popular recognition? Unfortunately, that's already one strike against your proposal. The fact that the overwhelming majority of authors aren't celebrities never figures into the equation. (I know—stupid, huh?) Neither does the fact that book publishers fail more often with built-in celebrity books than they succeed with them.[50] Nor the fact that publishers can actually *make you* a celebrity by publishing your book and investing marketing, publicity, and sales dollars into the promotion of it. In a publishing board meeting, those truths are irrelevant.

To the VP of sales, either you're a celebrity or you're not. If you are, he or she will be happy to vote in favor of publishing your book. And if you're not? Well, that could be the reason for your last rejection.

---

50 Truth is, celebrity books are notoriously expensive up front and require a huge marketing investment that may never pay off in the long run. Additionally, celebrity books typically have a short shelf-life in our ADHD-style society. Even a book with what could be considered significant sales for another author will often fail as a celebrity book, simply because there are too many frontloaded costs that can never be fully recouped by a publisher.

WHAT YOU CAN DO ABOUT IT...

1. Um...Quit writing and pursue a celebrity career?

Honestly, from a purely pragmatic perspective, this is the best advice for people who really just want to publish books without doing all that silly "writing" part. If that's you, then go ahead and get on *Survivor*, become a pro athlete, win *American Idol*, move to Los Angeles and become a movie or TV star, pursue fame as a YouTube sensation, fly to the moon, become a superhero, go partying with Paris Hilton, whatever you can do that will get you into the ranks of the notable and well-known. You'll never truly be an author, but hey, you'll get published, and that's what you want anyway, right?

Or you can...

2. Go back to Reason #33, and review strategies for building an author platform.

If you're not ready to abandon writing so you can become a celebrity and get published, then start thinking seriously about ways to improve your author platform.

By its nature, an author platform extends an author brand name. If you can extend your author brand to the point where it becomes a *brand/buy* name—a recognizable, and trusted, name that prompts people to buy—then you've achieved a measure of celebrity that will carry weight with both the sales and marketing VPs at a publishing house. Sure, you may never be as famous as Jay Leno or Paris Hilton, but that's OK. Minor celebrity that's translatable into brand/buy sales still makes a difference. A sales VP won't overlook the work you've done on the marketing side to build your author platform.

3. Get a few celebrities to endorse your book.

If you're not a celebrity yourself, you can still draw on the power of celebrity that a sales VP finds attractive. How? Get connected with a few celebs who might be willing to provide an endorsement for your book. This is, of course, easier said than done. But with celeb access through websites, Facebook, MySpace, Twitter, LinkedIn, and other options, it doesn't have to be impossible.

First, *don't* stalk a celebrity, either online or in person. I mean it. Just don't.

Next, try to connect with some of the people who are within your reach. Maybe through a friend or a friend of a friend. Maybe through a fan letter. Maybe through a note on a web blog, or through your agent or a shared editor. Maybe at a writer's conference or through a professor at film school. You get the idea.

True, most celebrities will probably ignore you. But if you can deliver even as few as two celebrity endorsements for your next book, the sales VP will definitely be interested—and it could be enough to tip that person's vote in your favor.

There Is No "Brandwagon"
Trend You Can Latch Onto

Remember back in 1999 when that whole "Y2K Virus!" end-of-the-world nonsense dominated everything? There were disaster novels and tech manuals and business books and more. That was a classic example of a "brand-wagon"—an overarching topic of interest to a broadly based audience, with multiple avenues for exploitation in product offerings. If your book connects to a current brandwagon, sales folks like that. If it doesn't have a brandwagon to ride on, that doesn't *guarantee* rejection...but it doesn't help sway salespeople in your favor either.

Think about it. When the *Lord of the Rings* trilogy was in theaters and the *Harry Potter* books were selling millions, there was a sudden glut of new fantasy authors and books that crowded bookstore shelves. Some of these copycats were great (the Percy Jackson series comes to mind); others—not so much. After 9/11, any book having to do with Osama Bin Laden or terrorism in general was suddenly a must-read. Then there was *The Da Vinci Code*, which spawned a cottage industry in *Da Vinci Code* response books. Then *The Purpose Driven Life* took over, and suddenly everything was some kind of "driven" (I particularly liked the title for women, *The Purse-Driven Life*). Then the *Twilight* saga took over and the world was full of undead people talking about their feelings. Then…well, you get the idea.

The lesson here is finding a hot topic and latching onto it with an associated book in time enough to profit from the fad before it fades. If (as we noted in Reason #54) you have the obvious bad luck of not being a celebrity, being able to brandwagon on an existing trend early in its development is a nice substitute. Why? Because the brandwagon fills the void left by your lack of an author brand name. Instead of celebrity, all you need is expertise or relevant association to the fad.

If, for instance, vampires are what readers are craving and you happen to be an authority on Vlad the Impaler, then your expertise might possibly be enough to cash in on the trend. Does it always work like this? No, of course not. But it does happen often enough that salespeople will definitely give a brandwagon book a second look.

I remember one time a certain book on prayer was dominating bestseller lists for an extended period of time. I was also working on a book about prayer, so I suggested to my editor that maybe we should change the title of my book to take advantage of the brandwagon effect. My publisher agreed and we were on our way.

Several months later news came out that two other publishers were also releasing books on prayer—with titles that were *exactly* the same as mine. And all were hitting bookstores within one month of each other. I panicked and asked to change the title of my book back to its original. Fortunately, my publisher disagreed. When the books came out, all three (mine included) hit industry bestseller lists. Brandwagon had carried the day—and that's why salespeople are often swayed by a brandwagon appeal.

Of course, the flip side of that equation is also true. If I've got a sales VP who has done homework in the market, he or she knows what kinds of trends are making money. If that sales VP is looking to cash in on some currently popular trend, and your book doesn't fit into any brandwagon opportunity, then that gives him or her yet another reason to reject your book. "Nobody's interested in this stuff," that VP will say. "What they really want are unicorns that talk about their feelings…"

Tough break, but that's the way it happens sometimes.

WHAT YOU CAN DO ABOUT IT…

1. Be a trend-watcher.

Pop culture defines America today the way a military culture defined ancient Rome or an agrarian culture defined the South during the Civil War. In ancient Rome, everybody knew what a soldier looked like. During the Civil War, every Southerner could talk comfortably about what it took to grow tobacco or cotton. And today, every American knows what happens on TV, in the theaters, and, to some extent, with the songs that are on the radio.

So pay attention to entertainment trends. Be on the lookout for big movie releases on the horizon. Read a variety of bestseller lists to try to spot topical trends that have real staying power. Listen at work to discover which TV shows people keep talking about. Basically, become a trend-watcher until you reach a point where you can predict the next big thing— and write a book to take advantage of the brandwagon opportunities that come with it.

2. Learn how to spot gaps.

Of course, it's not enough simply to spot a trend and then try to pile on with another book on that topic (see Reason #27). In order to effectively brandwagon a book, yours has to be a) somehow associated with the trend, and b) completely different from anything else associated with the trend. Yes, it's a delicate line to tread, but if you do it well, you can be very successful—and make your proposal something a sales team can't wait to get their hands on.

So learn how to spot gaps in the trend. Find those areas that are not yet being exploited, yet still fall within the scope of the popular theme. Be creative with that, and have fun. When you find that opening that no one else has yet to see, pounce on it as fast as you can.

An example: A few years ago I was acquiring nonfiction for a religious publisher. Everyone in the office kept talking about Jack Bauer and the TV show *24*. So I contacted one of my favorite authors and said, "Hey, what can you do that stays within copyright restrictions but also takes advantage of the popularity of *24*?" He came back to me with an idea for a book of short Bible studies inspired by season 1 of the TV show. No one had thought of studying the Bible by the light of the TV screen, or in the suspenseful shadow of Jack Bauer. The result? We published, and that book hit the Top 50 bestseller list for the Christian publishing industry.

3. Be more than a copycat artist.

Here's one important caveat about trying to brandwagon your way to success: *No copycats.*

There's a difference between being a copycat and identifying a trend, spotting a gap in the market associated with that trend, and filling it with a related, but truly original, book product. If you don't know that difference, then *don't* try to brandwagon a book (and re-read Reason #27). At no time should anyone be able to say that yours is simply a "copycat" of someone else's work. That's both unappealing and possibly illegal as a violation of copyright protections.

For instance, at the beginning of the twenty-first century, the world already had Harry Potter. We didn't need (or want) "Henry Powers, Wizard Boy." But Percy Jackson, son of the

Olympian god Poseidon? Well, him we couldn't wait to meet— and the rest was history (or mythstory, or…you get the idea!). So even though you are riding the coattails of some other trend, make sure you avoid the temptation to copycat that trend. Again, it's a fine line…but one that could mean the difference between a publishing contract and just another rejection letter to add to your growing collection.

{ Reason № 56 }

You Have No Sales History to Speak Of

Every time my sales VP casts a vote in favor of a new book, he or she is placing a big-money bet. And you can bet that VP is very aware of what's at stake.

Look at it this way: Imagine you and I jet off to Las Vegas in time to place a bet on a horserace happening at Churchill Downs. We're watching the pre-race coverage on TV, learning about the horses scheduled to run in the race. One is a horse named HotStuff. As we listen to the announcer, we discover that HotStuff placed third in a race six months ago, came in first three months ago, and was barely edged out of the top spot to finish second in a race just last month.

Next we hear the announcer introduce a horse named CoolIt. CoolIt, we discover, has never raced before. He looks healthy, but no one knows exactly how this horse will respond once he's on the track. Will CoolIt panic and freeze up? Will the horse brush off all distractions and race hard to the finish line? Will he simply stay in the middle of the pack, never making an impact on the race? Who knows?

Now it's time for you and me to go to the betting window and put our money down on a horse. Realistically, are you going to bet $25,000, $50,000, or more on CoolIt? Or are you going to look at the track records of the two horses and go with the safer bet on HotStuff?

When I come to the publishing board with a book by an author who has never sold any books before, I'm asking my sales VP to do the equivalent of placing a bet on CoolIt— putting money behind an author who may look healthy but who has no history of success. She's placing a bet of tens of thousands of dollars (sometimes more) on the hope that your masterpiece will win, place, or show in the race at the public marketplace. That's a pretty risky bet, and it's one that makes it hard for brand-new authors to even get in the game. Mick Silva spent several years as an editor at Random House's Waterbrook Multnomah division, and he says, "Publishers, retailers, and parent companies are taking losses, so they're backing off making bets."[51]

The rule is this, then: Past sales success creates future opportunities; no past creates only uncertainty. And most times, that's enough for rejection.

---

51 Steve Rabey, "Publishing's New Paradigm," *Evangel* (June 6, 2010), 22.

WHAT YOU CAN DO ABOUT IT...

1. Bolster your credibility as an expert to overcome your lack of credibility as an author.

Stellar author credentials can often help first-timers overcome the absence of a track record in book sales simply because a recognized "expert" is someone readers inherently trust. If you lack a sales history, then beef up your author credentials on your book's topic and use that to convince my sales VP you're worthy of her bet.

For instance, Audrey Niffenegger had never published anything when she pitched her fantasy novel, *The Time-Traveler's Wife*, to MacAdam/Cage. But she was a well-regarded professor in the Interdisciplinary Book Arts MFA program at the prestigious Columbia College Chicago Center for Book and Paper Arts[52]—and that's significant. In horseracing parlance, that kind of credential was like saying she came from a family of racing champions. In fact, I'd guess that without that credential, Ms. Niffenegger might never have been published.

So identify key accomplishments that make you a credible expert on a topic, and highlight those in your proposal. That'll help mitigate some of the risk for my sales team.

---

52 Audrey Niffenegger, *The Time-Traveler's Wife* (San Francisco: MacAdam/Cage, 2003), back flap.

2. Try to publish in categories where the topic is more important than the author.

Some categories of publishing almost always require author brand recognition for success—literary fiction, mysteries/thrillers, memoir, etc. Sure, an unknown author can sometimes break through there, but it's rare. Other categories depend more on built-in topic appeal—such as romantic fiction, crafts, home and garden, finance, and some children's or teen books.

When choosing where you want to start your publishing career, one option is to find a category that doesn't require a previous sales history, or a category where your other credentials matter more. For instance, if your day job is as a financial planner, you may want to try to break into publishing with a money management book. Or, if you want to pursue a career as a novelist, you may want to start by writing romance to build up a history of sales.

3. Highlight your ability to reach a significant audience.

In the end, the most important thing to a sales VP is going to be your ability to sell books, regardless of what your past history has been. So look for ways to tell that VP your book will definitely sell—maybe through your 10,000-member mailing list, at the 200 speaking engagements you've got scheduled next year, through your magazine column that reaches 150,000 readers every month, or whatever.

{ Reason № 57 }

You Have a Sales History, and It Sucks

It's tempting, sometimes, to think that just being published is enough for success in a writing career. Unfortunately, there are times when *being* published can actually be an obstacle to *getting* published. This is particularly true if you decide to pursue self-publishing as a shortcut to jump-starting your career.

Here's a rule of thumb: any book of yours that sells less than 10,000 copies is going to be considered a failure.

That seems harsh, I know. Especially considering the general opinion is that most books will only sell around 5,000 copies anyway, and most often selling those 5,000 copies will still be enough for a book to be reasonably profitable. But even a book that sells 10,000 copies isn't necessarily considered a success; it's just not thought of as a failure anymore.

As an agent, if you send me a proposal and tell me you've published in the past, I'm going to ask for specific unit sales figures on those previous books. Why? Because I know any editor worth her salt out there is going to ask me for that same information. I'm hoping to see one or two books that sold more than 20,000 copies (generally considered a success in publishing), but I'll still be OK if you're typically selling 10,000 copies of each book you publish. If none of your books gets close to that, I'm going to have to decline the opportunity to represent, just because your track history has proven that people aren't terribly interested in buying your books.

This is one of those rules of publishing success I hate, and which hits home for me. I represent someone I believe to be an immensely talented suspense novelist. Her fans think she's the next Dean Koontz, and she's actually won a national award for her writing. But she's published three novels to date—two of them with publishing behemoth Simon & Schuster—and none of her books has sold more than 6,000 copies.

That's just not enough in a crowded marketplace like fiction publishing. I can't sell her fourth book, and S&S dropped her even before her third novel released, citing low sales of her second book as the reason.

So you see, sometimes a little success in publishing is worse than no success at all.

WHAT YOU CAN DO ABOUT IT...
1. Omit what you don't like.
If you've published in the past, and unit sales numbers from those previous endeavors aren't impressive, then just don't tell me about those books. Don't mention them at all—maybe I

won't notice. You'll still have to deal with the perception that you have no sales history to speak of (see Reason #56), but that's better than telling me that your sales history sucks.

Some authors think that any published book is something to be proud of, and they insist on listing everything they've ever done. This is your ego talking, so ignore it. Be sure to tell me about *only* the books that make you look good. For instance, I've published more than forty books myself, but if you read any bio of me anywhere, you'll see—at the maximum—that I list only about half of those books. And most often I'll just list three to five of my top sellers. Why? Well, obviously, the ones I've omitted were, um, a bit *less* than successful in the marketplace. Some books you trumpet, others you bury. So be sure to bury the ones that don't flatter you.

2. If you just can't avoid talking about it, then highlight what you learned about how to make a book successful.

If you're pressed by an editor or agent who wants to know why your book (or books) failed in the marketplace, *don't* try to shift the blame to others. (Hey, we all know your books got no marketing support, but we won't accept that as an excuse anyway.) Instead, present it as a learning experience that will make your next book's prospects that much better.

Talk about the inexperience of youth, the carelessness of innocence, or whatever. And tell a few specific ways you'll "change" in order to help your publisher sell your next book. Make it clear you want to avoid going through that poor sales "learning experience" again.

For instance, you might say something like this: "With my last book, I was still early in my writing career. I took the idea of success for granted—and I paid the price for it. From that experience, I've learned that I really need to be a strong partner for my publisher, both in the writing and in promotion of my book. So for this next book, I'm planning to do a much better job as a publishing partner. Specifically, I will…"

Make sense?

3. Cultivate ways to increase sales of your existing books.

This is so hard to do without the assistance of a big-pocket partner (like, say, a publishing house's sales team), but since current sales affect future opportunities, it may be worth your while to stop writing for a year or so and invest your time and money into bolstering sales of your books that are already on the market.

No, this won't be easy. And you may fail miserably at it. But if you succeed, it will definitely help your chances for the future in the eyes of my sales VP.

{ Reason № 58 }

You Self-Published Yourself into Oblivion

These words of noted author, radio personality, and columnist Garrison Keillor sound ominously familiar, do they not?

> *The future of publishing: eighteen million authors in America, each with an average of fourteen readers, eight of whom are blood relatives. Average annual earnings: $1.75.*[53]

With the proliferation of print-on-demand (POD) technology and the growing affordability of self-publishing options, the previously sequestered ability to print a book has never been more widely available to anyone, anywhere. As long as you can write a check to a self-publishing company, you can publish pretty much anything you like.

Or, as the venerable Mr. Keillor puts it, "The upside of self-publishing is that you can write whatever you wish, utter

---

53   Garrison Keillor, "The End of an Era in Publishing," *New York Times* online, (May 26, 2010).

freedom, and that is also the downside. You can write whatever you wish and everyone in the world can exercise their right to read the first three sentences and delete the rest."[54]

I know. That seems a touch unkind.

After all, what does an elitist author like Garrison Keillor know about your struggles to achieve your vision of a writing career? You've gotten dozens of rejection letters for your book recently. Agents and editors alike are determinedly indifferent to your prose and your dreams. Self-publishing is affordable— finally—and it gives you an opportunity to prove your worth by delivering an actual, physical book to show off in the marketplace. Why not give that a shot, since traditional methods aren't working for you anyway?

Here's the catch: Publishing a book and *successfully* publishing a book are remarkably different things—especially in the eyes of my sales VP and his team. My sales team doesn't give a rat's tailswing that you've published a book. They only care if you can publish *a book that'll sell*. Self-publishing yourself into oblivion does nothing to prove that to them.

Just last week I received a query from an author who listed two previously published books in his credits. Knowing I was going to write this chapter, I checked Amazon.com to learn more about his work. Both books had been self-published on

---

54 Garrison Keillor, "The End of an Era in Publishing," *New York Times* online, (May 26, 2010).

Lulu.com. One ranked a miserable 4,621,308 on Amazon. The other ranked at 4,810,589.

I'm sure this author thought he was helping his career when he sent those books into the Lulu system, but he wasn't. The abysmal sales history he earned as a result of his self-publishing efforts was enough for me to send an easy rejection.

Consider yourself warned.

WHAT YOU CAN DO ABOUT IT...

1. Don't self-publish as a stepping-stone toward success in traditional publishing.

This may seem counterintuitive to some, but if you want to publish, don't self-publish. That is, if your ultimate goal is a career in traditional publishing channels, don't try to short-cut your way to success by self-publishing one market failure after another.

Despite the fact that self-publishing works by entirely different standards than traditional publishing, any book that's in the marketplace will be judged by the same expectations that my sales VP has for books he publishes. That means you could legitimately self-publish and be wildly successful in that effort with sales of 700 or 800 copies of your book. But when my sales VP sees that you have a book in print with only 800 in sales, he'll view that as abysmal and as proof that you are unsalable on a larger scale.

So, unless you can guarantee yourself a significant number

of sales, or unless you don't care about pursuing a traditional publishing career, just don't self-publish. You'll do yourself more harm than good otherwise.

2. Self-publish for personal reasons, not for professional ones.

OK, lest you think I am unfairly exclusive and judgmental about self-publishing, I will admit there are a few good reasons to pursue a POD opportunity for your book. Those reasons have nothing to do with traditional book publishing success, though. Still, if you don't care about becoming a career author or about someday pursuing publication through a traditional publishing house, then sure, self-publishing could be a good option for you.

For instance, if you want to tell your life story and leave it behind as a legacy gift for your kids and grandkids—well, that sounds pretty cool to me. Or if you want to create a keepsake book of poetry and stories for family and friends, then by all means, print up a dozen copies and send them out this Christmas. Or if you want to put together a fun little advice book for newlyweds and give it as a wedding gift every time kids in your church get married, well, that's just sweet, so why not?

So, yes, there are plenty of personal, relational reasons to self-publish a book. If that's your motivation, then go right ahead…just don't assume that it will lead to professional success as a result.

3. If you've already self-published for the wrong reason, slant it as an "educational" experience.

There is value for an absolute novice writer to go through the self-publishing process as an educational tool. Doing so gives you a hands-on, practice education on the unique requirements and daily demands of a publishing enterprise. It helps you better understand a traditional publishing process because now you know what's needed editorially, promotionally, and production-wise to create a final product. And afterward, you can exploit what you've learned to become a much better author partner for any traditional publishing house that chooses to start your "real" author career.

At least that's what you can tell an editor who asks about your abysmal sales after your preemptive attempt at self-publishing. (Good luck.)

{ Reason № 59 }

Women Just Aren't That Into You

A few years ago, I attended a writer's conference in Colorado. During the day, I had conversations with several men who whined about their lack of success breaking into the publishing business. They seemed truly mystified that companies out there were giving their books a steady stream of rejection letters.

Later in the day, I had some free time so I decided to attend one of the workshops taught by another speaker. I chose "Writing for Women." When that seminar started, it became crystal clear for me why all the other men I'd talked to previously were having such trouble in publishing. You see, I was the only male present in the "Writing for Women" seminar. What's odd is that some people thought it was odd for me to be there.

That's fine. I'll take that oddity all the way to the bank.

Here's the reality: Women dictate buying in America. You'd better understand that if you want a career in publishing. Consider the numbers:

- Women make up more than half the population.[55]
- Women buy more books than men.[56]
- American women control $4.3 trillion of annual spending in the U.S. economy—more than the entire annual spending of China and India combined.[57]
- Women earn more bachelor's degrees than men, which projects to mean that their earning power will actually *increase* in years to come.[58]
- Women influence 80 percent of the buying decisions in the United States.[59]

Read that last number again…did that say *80 percent*? Why yes, I believe it did. And yet you've never thought too much about writing for women? About making sure any book you write has some kind of "woman appeal"? Well, no wonder you're reading this book instead of having published dozens of your own.

---

55 Bridget Brennan, *Why She Buys* (New York: Crown Business, 2009), 267.

56 Pamela N. Danziger, *Why People Buy Things They Don't Need* (Chicago, IL: Dearborn Trade Publishing, 2004), 151.

57 Michael J. Silverstein and Kate Sayre, "The Female Economy," *Harvard Business Review* (September 2009), 3, 7.

58 Brennan, 31.

59 Brennan, 29.

WHAT YOU CAN DO ABOUT IT...

1. Follow the money (knock on the even-numbered doors).

Remember this rule: 80 percent of your readers are women, 20 percent are everybody else. So when creating a new proposal, you'd better ask yourself how women will respond to your book.

Look at it this way: Assume you're a door-to-door salesperson, and your territory is one apartment building in New York City. In every odd-numbered apartment there lives a person with $20 to spend. In every even-numbered apartment there lives a person with $80 to spend. Are you going to knock on the odd-numbered doors first, or the even-numbered doors?

You can bet my sales VP is going to knock on the even-numbered doors, because that's where 80 percent of the money is. So follow the money and make sure your book has something women want. A few books to help you with this are *Why She Buys* by Bridget Brennan and *Don't Think Pink* by Lisa Johnson and Andrea Learned.

2. Be aware of the six "basic archetypes" of female consumers.

I'm indebted to Michael J. Silverstein and Kate Sayre's excellent report, "The Female Economy," for identifying these archetypes, "which are primarily defined by income, age, and stage of life."[60] They are

- Fast-Tracker (independent woman, striving for achievement)
- Pressure Cooker (successful multitasker, struggling for stability)
- Relationship Focused (middle class, married with kids)
- Managing on Her Own (single, divorced, or widowed, seeking connection)
- Fulfilled Empty Nester (concerned about health, travel, leisure)
- Making Ends Meet (lower income, less educated, seeks value and small luxuries)

Be aware that these archetypes can overlap for many women, but if you write a book that appeals to women in one or more of these life circumstances, you're increasing exponentially the chances that your book will sell in the marketplace. That's something my sales VP will be happy to hear.

---

60   Michael J. Silverstein and Kate Sayre, "The Female Economy," *Harvard Business Review* (September 2009), 4.

3. Don't assume that because you are a woman you can innately write for women. And don't assume being a man means you can't write for women.

Being born a certain gender may give you advantages in life and may even help your publishing career. But it's idiotic to assume that all women can write for women or that no man can write for a woman. Don't allow that kind of gender bias to dictate what you do in writing.

The best writers—male or female—are knowledgeable, articulate, and interesting. So while you must never lose sight of the fact that a woman is your most likely reader, you must also understand that the number of X and Y chromosomes you have doesn't determine your ability to be successful as a writer. Writing is equal opportunity bloodsport.

{ Reason № 60 }

My Sales VP Thinks of You as an Unknown (the "No Froofies" Rule)

Ah, the curse of anonymity. This has killed many a writer's career.

I once knew an editor who labeled all authors in one of two categories: froofy and non-froofy. (I know, we editors are an articulate bunch, are we not?)

This editor perceived froofy writers as uneducated, under-employed, random nobodies who'd once read a book and decided to give writing a shot. Non-froofy writers were, well, people like you, dear reader, with sincere skill and promise for publication. (Hey, every writer's got to suck up to the reader sometimes, right?)

Although they don't typically use the word "froofy," all sales VPs think in terms of that duality. And if you're a gener-ally unknown writer suffering under the curse of anonymity, that means you're a "froofy" in her eyes.

Look at it this way: Let's say you work in bookstore sales at my publishing house. Your job is to convince book buyers at Barnes & Noble to carry our books. You have two books to sell today. Both have exactly the same title and exactly the same cover image. One is written by the president of the United States. The other is written by, well, you.

Which book are you going to have more success selling? Right.

It's nothing personal, you see. My sales VP is just thinking about all those industrious salespeople who earn their living by working for her. She's responsible for giving them the tools they need to succeed. If she gives them a book by an absolute "nobody," they're going to have a hard time making money from it. And if they don't succeed, my sales VP won't succeed.

So, whether she admits it out loud or not, she's adopted a "no froofies" rule toward every book. If she sees you as an unknown entity, that's enough to earn you a rejection, plain and simple.

WHAT YOU CAN DO ABOUT IT...

1. Become known.

I'm not saying you must become a celebrity before you can publish (though, according to Reason #54, that certainly helps). But I am saying that if you're seeking a public career like that of an author, you probably should also be making a name for yourself somewhere, in some way.

No, don't break the law or do some stupid publicity stunt (Balloon Boy, anyone?). But do become a recognized expert in your field. Look for opportunities to be a public speaker.

Be a notable contributor to a popular website. Start your own website or blog. Star in a local theater production. Enter writing contests—and win them. Take steps that bring you broader and broader exposure in the public eye.

For help in this area, check out Christina Katz's practical advice in *Get Known Before the Book Deal*.

2. Highlight your public accomplishments in your proposal.

After you've done some of the things in suggestion #1 above, be sure to tell me about them! The best place for this is in your author bio, but you can also include these kinds of things in your personal publicity and marketing plan.

For instance, you might mention that you frequently perform at The Cool House Theater in your local community, and that gives you an avenue to include an ad for your book in the theater program, which is distributed to 7,500 people over the course of a normal production run.

Whatever it is you are known for, just make sure I know about it. Then when my sales VP asks me, "So who is this person anyway?" I'll have something to say besides, "Oh, she's some nobody in western Illinois. But she's a good writer. Promise."

3. Learn how to write press releases.

This is an overlooked skill among writers, but the ability to create a short, professional-looking press release is often a good way to tout your own accomplishments. You can even go ahead and send it to your local newspapers and media outlets—maybe even get coverage in those places. If you do, include any relevant clippings in your proposal. But even if you don't get coverage, you can still include a press release or two with your proposal. I may toss it aside…but then I may look at it and be impressed as well.

I knew an author once who made it a habit to send out a press release about himself and his writing career at least twice a year. His mailing list was the thirty or forty editors he hoped to work with someday in the future. He didn't pitch any books or ask for any consideration when he sent those press releases. He said their whole purpose was simply to put his name regularly in the minds of editors. He felt that if an editor recognized his name when a new proposal came in— regardless of whether she knew why she recognized it—that meant he'd no longer be considered a nobody at the publishing house. You might consider doing something similar with your own press releases.

My Sales VP Is Hostile toward Me or My Editorial VP, and Is Sabotaging Our Careers by Undervaluing Proposals We Bring to Publishing Board

I'd love to tell you that publishing board represents an ideal of democratic process and respectful restraint…but it just doesn't.

Sometimes, I have to admit, a publishing board meeting resembles a rowdy soccer match—except that we're not blowing on vuvuzela horns. Oh sure, we try to get along—after all, we have to work together every day. But sometimes tempers flare, grudges form, and well, you can guess the rest.

I still remember vividly a time when I managed to anger a production VP during a publishing board meeting. OK, I didn't call him a flat-out liar, but I did suggest that perhaps his version of the truth wasn't consistent with reality. The guy was huge—ex-military, all crew cut and biceps. He promptly let me know he'd be happy to walk with me to the parking lot where his fists would show me his truth. (I politely declined. Yikes!)

Other times I've sat silently by and watched as shouting matches raged between editorial directors and sales VPs, when people stormed out of the room in protest, and when we all just had to take a break because we were exhausted from arguing.

But I'll tell you, those obvious confrontations are much desired over the ones that simmer below the surface. I once had a sales VP approach me and practically beg me to put together a proposal for a certain project. He guaranteed it would pass because his sales team would support it 100 percent. So I did what he'd asked for.

Then, during publishing board, when all the executives were present, he delivered a complete 180-degree opposite argument, using my proposal (that he'd shaped and requested!) as a tool for belittling my boss and the "inadequate ideas" we were supposedly trying to foist on his sales team.

Ouch.

Now, to be honest, these situations I've described are always the exception, not the rule. Most of the time, most publishing people are consummate professionals—including the two jerks I mentioned above. Still, if you've worked in any office environment at all, you know that politics and posturing run rampant in the hallways—especially among executives with big egos and much to gain or lose.

Why do I tell you this? Because it's possible that the rejection letter you received yesterday was actually undeserved. It's rare, but it could be that you were the collateral damage of some unseen pissing contest going on at the highest levels in my publishing company.

So, you know, sorry about that.

WHAT YOU CAN DO ABOUT IT...

1. Stay out of the fray.

Look, I told you about this reason for rejection just because it exists, not because I expect you to actually get involved in a fight between a sales VP and your editorial contact. If you hear of a conflict brewing in the management team at a publishing house, just don't pick sides. Don't commiserate with your editor and send an email complaining about those shortsighted folks in sales. Don't try to defend the sales team to your editor. Just accept the news and then ignore it.

Although political turf wars in a publishing house may affect your business (whether or not you're able to publish), they're really none of your business. It's a family affair, and you're not in the family. So just stay above the fray and avoid saying or doing anything that appears to make you choose sides.

2. Get along with the sales team.

If you have an opportunity to meet members of a publishing house's sales team—say, at a BookExpo America convention, or during a tour of a publishing company, or whatever—be sure to suck up a little bit. Don't be insincere, of course, but do treat these people with respect and regard. Take time to admire the quality of their work, especially under difficult circumstances. Ask what an author like you could do to make their jobs easier. Generally be the kind of person salespeople like. That makes life easier for you—and for your editor.

3. Be better than the politics.

The best way to overcome a sabotaging spirit within a publishing house is to come up with a proposal that's such a can't-miss project, no one in his or her right mind would turn it down.

If you're thinking like my sales VP (and you should be), then you can manipulate my sales VP into liking your proposal in spite of her personal dislike for me or my boss. Make your book something that's so salesworthy that she'd actually be harming her whole department—and her own career—in order to strike out at me by rejecting it.

Hey, excellence trumps pettiness every time. So be excellent. Period.

{ Reason № 62 }

My Sales VP Can't (or Won't) See the Future

The publishing business would be a lot easier if fortune-tellers really could predict the future. Then all we'd have to do is put a few on the payroll and let them tell us what will sell like Panera bread eighteen months from now.

Alas, the real world is not so easy. Instead we've got all kinds of people trying to predict what the next big book will be. There's you, of course, studying the market and creating a book to meet future trends. There's me, sitting at my agency desk, aggregating all my resources to uncover that elusive next bestseller. There's the editor trying to duplicate past successes while avoiding present failures. And there's my sales VP, adding up the numbers each month to get a sense of what's selling now and how to sell more of it.

Trouble is, most often we all arrive at different conclusions. And when it comes to the perspective of a sales professional, the big concern is what's selling today—not trying to predict what will sell tomorrow.

So what happens if you come to me with a truly visionary

book idea, one that is timed perfectly to exploit an as-yet-under-the-radar trend destined to explode just in time for your prospective book's release?

This is where it gets tricky. My sales VP is very much aware of what's selling *right now*, and he likely hasn't put on his seer spectacles to peer terribly far into the future. Before the 2002 release of the first Spider-Man film, I remember trying to talk up the future of superhero-themed products to some of my industry colleagues. "That stuff is niche material for kids," the sales folks told me. "It's not for an everyday book buyer. Pass."

Well, if you've been alive since 2002, you know what happened after that. Major movies like *Spider-Man* (1, 2, and 3), the X-Men franchise, *Batman Begins*, *Iron Man*, *The Dark Knight*, and more have dominated pop culture for nearly a decade. And if you look on bookstore shelves, there are gobs of superhero-themed titles vying for our money—many of which are selling very well.

But I couldn't make sales teams see the future in that area, so they—and I—missed out on the trend.

What does that mean for you? Well, you may spot a trend with plenty of time to capitalize on it…and you may still get rejected because my sales VP simply can't take her eyes off today long enough to catch the vision for tomorrow.

WHAT YOU CAN DO ABOUT IT...

1. Show clear data to support your vision.

One thing you can rely on with a sales VP is that numbers will count. If you spot a trend that appears to have profit potential in the future, start translating that trend into numbers. Talk about where we are today and how that projects out for the future. Speak the language of population figures, similar sales trends, charts, and graphs.

If you can back up your instincts with data that supports your trend analysis, my sales VP will listen. If your numbers are accurate and project a strong return on investment, my VP might just say yes to your book after all.

2. Don't stop pitching.

If you see a profitable potential coming in the future, don't give up when the trend becomes obvious. Keep pitching your ideas, finding new publishers, and reiterating your data to anyone who will listen.

Hey, if your predictions are correct, you'll start to see evidence of that in the marketplace—and so will the suits at the publishing companies. At some point, your prediction will hit a tipping point where everyone is aware of it. And if your book proposal is sitting on an editor's desk when a sales VP finally notices the trend and tells the editorial department about it, you're in a good spot to be the one who profits from it.

3. Diversify.

Be ready to capitalize on several future trends—not just one. If you try to convince my sales VP that certain products will boom eighteen months from now, and he doesn't believe you, go ahead and file those ideas away for the moment. Then tackle the next upcoming trend on your list and pitch new ideas related to that one. Keep delivering diversified targets in your proposals, and sooner or later one is likely to make an impact.

The worst idea is the one that keeps getting rehashed, so think of yourself as a library of great ideas, not a shrine to a single one.

{ Reason № 63 }

You Are the Wrong Gender

I know an author—let's call him Ben—who wrote an award-winning inspirational book for women. Of course, the women who read that book (including the folks who bestowed the award) have no idea Ben wrote it.

"When I started looking at similar books in the market," Ben told me privately, "I realized they were all written for women by women. Well, one of my relatives—a woman—is also an author. So I contacted her and asked if I could borrow her name in order to publish my book. She agreed, so I ghostwrote the book under her name. She got the byline. I got to publish a book I felt passionately about. Seemed like a fair deal to me."

Yes, Virginia, there is a gender bias in publishing.

Now, before you get all pointy and self-righteous about the fact that a guy has to ghostwrite a book under a woman's name in order to get published, please be aware that the gender bias that governs many book decisions didn't originate inside the publishing house. It's simply a reflection of bias in the marketplace. If the majority of readers didn't assume men were generally inadequate in addressing female issues, my sales team wouldn't either. But money runs the world, and if your money says no to a male author, well, I'd better go get a female author.

Of course not every publishing category has to deal with gender bias. Thanks to barrier-busting careers of people like Agatha Christie, Ursula K. Le Guin, Suze Orman, and others, women have easily gained widespread credibility in areas once dominated by men, and vice versa.

Ah, but when was the last time you saw a woman's name attached to a book on trout fishing? Or a man's name on the cover of a romance novel? Or a woman's byline on a super-hero comic or graphic novel? Heck, it wasn't until 2007 that DC Comics finally assigned a woman—lauded author Gail Simone—to be the regular, long-term writer for Wonder Woman, their most famous *female* superhero of all time.[61]

The fact is that in some book categories, readers expect the author to be a certain gender. And that means my sales VP does too.

If you happen to be someone trying to buck that kind of publishing expectation—say, a man writing about beauty and fashion, or a woman writing about the greatest linebackers of the NFL—you've got an uphill battle ahead of you. Your gender alone may be enough to make my sales VP decline your book.

---

61   The Linster, "Gail Simone restores the wonder to Wonder Woman," AfterEllen.com.

WHAT YOU CAN DO ABOUT IT...

1. Try writing under your initials instead of your full first name.

Some people have had success simply adopting a pseudonym (George Orwell is a classic example of this), but I think the better option is simply to keep your own name and present it in gender-neutral terms, using your first and middle initials in place of your full first name.

For instance, I once published a female suspense author named Tracy. For her byline, she preferred to use the initials "T.L." in place of her first name. This practice is pretty common actually, and it operates on the assumption that readers will assign their own gender preferences to the neutral initials. Sometimes that can be enough to remove a reader's bias long enough for that person to buy your book—which means it may also be enough to eliminate gender as an obstacle for my sales VP.

2. Consider a coauthor of the opposite gender.

I know a male fiction author who writes very good romance novels. But he couldn't get published in that genre on his own. So he teamed up with a female romance novelist to publish a few love stories. The tactic worked, and he had significant success writing in that genre for a few years before moving on to something else.

However, you should be aware that this strategy also has its drawbacks. For instance, the male author I mentioned above ended up writing 90 percent of the books he "coauthored" with the female romance novelist, and when they finally parted ways, it was not as friends. Additionally, coauthoring a book requires a genuine collaborative spirit, which is often difficult if you are the person who came up with the original idea.

So, in the end, I can't say I'd recommend this strategy for everyone. But the truth is that it can sometimes work. Your call.

3. Viva la différence! (Long live the difference!)

Another tactic to overcome this obstacle is to emphasize it so that this perceived weakness becomes almost a history-making strength unique to your project.

For instance, if you're a man writing tips for growing prize-winning gardenias, you might title your book *There's a Guy in the Garden (And It's about Time!)*. Or if you're a woman writing about how the internal combustion engine works, you could tout yourself as "one of America's leading female mechanics!"

One of my favorite books of recent years (which I actually bought!) is *The Bad Ass Girl's Guide to Poker: All You Need to Beat the Boys* by Toby Leah Bochan. Ms. Bochan is definitely a woman in a man's world when it comes to tournament poker—and she turned that perceived weakness into a bona fide strength with creativity and attitude. I loved it, and apparently, so did the people who published her book.

Yes, this approach can be risky, but if done well, it can also make a big difference in the way my sales VP views your book's publishing potential.

{ Reason № 64 }

You Have Unrealistic Expectations about Your Publishing Potential

I always laugh when I watch a movie about writers. Inevitably in movies, the very first book a writer creates gets immediately published and becomes an instant bestseller regardless of whether it's a silly pop-up book (*Throw Momma from the Train*), a self-help psychology book (*What about Bob?*), or anything else thrust on the public in that fictional world.

Well, I've got bad news for you: Life ain't like the movies. Sorry.

If you come to me with an inflated ego and sky-high expectations, regardless of the quality of your book, I'm going to reject you. (Hey, my ego is bigger than yours anyway, right?)

A few years ago I got a proposal from a small-college professor that I really liked. It was for a niche audience, but I figured it was still strong enough that a publisher in that category would be able to sell at least 10,000 copies. That would be a strong beginning for this first-time author, so I started talking with him about possibilities. I asked one of my standard questions: "What are your expectations with this book?"

With a straight face, he answered, "Well, Rick Warren sold several million copies of *The Purpose Driven Life*, so I expect my book to sell at least that."

My jaw dropped.

First-time author…publishing in a niche category…and he expected me to turn his writing debut into a book that would compete for the title of *bestselling hardcover nonfiction title in publishing history*?[62] Whaa?

The truth is, more than a million books are published each year,[63] and only about 250 manage to make it onto one of the *New York Times* bestseller lists during that time.[64] That means the odds of his book hitting a *NYT* list were, at best, 4,200 to one. He's twenty times more likely to marry a millionaire (odds at about 215 to 1) than to write a bestselling book—let alone make publishing sales history.[65]

I tried to explain to this author the mathematical realities of publishing in his category—and to point out the huge differences between him and Rick Warren, but he would have nothing to do with it. Finally I just gave up and walked away. To my knowledge, his book has never been published.

The lesson for you is this: if you want to publish your book,

---

62 "Rick Warren's New Book Delayed Again," *Christian Retailing*, www.christianretailing.com.

63 "New Book Titles and Editions, 2002–2009," BowkerInfo.com.

64 Gregory Baer, *Life: The Odds* (New York: Gotham Books, 2003), 49.

65 Gregory Baer, 16.

you must be realistic about its potential. Don't assume that you are entitled to the same success as some other popular publishing phenomenon out there, or demand to be treated like a *New York Times* bestseller before you've become a *New York Times* bestseller. All that does is show people like me that you are an egotistical rube who knows nothing about the realities of a writing career. And that means my rejection letter will soon land in your mailbox.

WHAT YOU CAN DO ABOUT IT...

1. Don't let your ego define you.

Honestly, I know that anyone who aspires to a career in publishing must have a rather significant ego. Let's face it, it takes a certain hefty amount of narcissism to assume that thousands, if not millions, of people should read your words like precious pearls—paying you for the privilege to do so.

That said, it's a mistake to let your ego define you, or to let your ambitions be the sole motivation for your actions. Arrogance is never attractive, and unearned arrogance is always opposed. So, when it comes time to move into a paying career as a writer, be careful not to let your ego be the thing that defines you in the eyes of an editor or agent.

Take pride in the quality of your work, not in the as-yet-unseen outcome of your publishing endeavor. Then you'll be successful regardless of how many copies your book sells.

2. Choose your benchmarks wisely.

Tom Brady is one of the best NFL quarterbacks of all time. He's won three Super Bowls with the New England Patriots and seems to be in the hunt for a fourth championship ring just about every season. Plus, he's married to one of the most beautiful women in the world.

Now, if you've never played pro sports, is it realistic for you to expect to step onto any football field and immediately experience the same kind of success that Tom Brady has? Of course not! Heck, Peyton Manning (of the Indianapolis Colts) is every bit as skilled as Tom Brady—yet as of 2010, Peyton had only one championship to Mr. Brady's three.

The lesson here is one of benchmarking. Yes, it's good to seek inspiration in your career from others who have achieved extreme success. At the same time, it's unwise to assume because someone else has reached the pinnacle that you are next in line. You simply can't compare yourself to J.K. Rowling or Rick Warren or Kitty Kelley until you've achieved success similar to Rowling, Warren, Kelley, or anyone.

So choose your benchmarks wisely. Find where you might fit on the ladder of publishing in your current circumstance, and aim for there to start. Once you achieve that success, aim for the next rung, and keep climbing one rung at a time until you reach the top. Then other people will waste time comparing themselves to you.

3. Treat yourself like someone else.

One of my gifts is the ability to assess a manuscript w
cold, critical eye. If I couldn't do that, I certainly wouldn't su
ceed as an agent or a writer. Imagine if I only used that gift
on *other people's* manuscripts...There's no way I would have
stuck around in this business for the past twenty-plus years!

Even with this very book, I must periodically stop and
evaluate it against the standards of the industry. The way I do
that is to first divorce myself from my past successes, from my
hopes for the future, from anything except the words in front
of my face. After all, that's all you're going to know of me when
you read this book.

In short, I must treat myself like I'd treat someone else—
with a cold, critical assessment that demands excellence without insisting on the rewards I hope will come with it. I'm going
to be honest: I don't always achieve that goal. But as long as
I'm trying, my work will stand out from the crowd. Unless,
of course, you do the same thing too. Then I'll probably have
some stiff competition.

№ 65 }

You Don't Know Why People Buy Books

Here's a pop quiz for you: Consumer behavior experts identify fourteen "justifiers" people use to convince themselves that it's OK to buy something. How many of those can you name?

Ready…go.

Done so soon?

Here are the correct answers, based on Pamela Danziger's consumer buying research through Unity Marketing:[66]

- Quality of Life
- ◉ Pleasure
- Home Beautification
- Education
- ◉ Relaxation
- ◉ Entertainment
- Planned Purchase

---

66 Pamela N. Danziger, *Why People Buy Things They Don't Need* (Chicago, IL: Dearborn Trade Publishing, 2004), 61.

- ◉ Emotional Satisfaction
- ◉ Existing Item Replacement
- ◉ Stress Relief
- • Hobby
- ◉ Gift for Self
- • Bought on Impulse
- • Status

How many justifiers did you come up with? All fourteen? Ten? Five? One?

Chances are, even if you got some right, you simply guessed at what they were. Chances are also good that my sales VP is intimately acquainted with the majority of the items on this list. She has to be, because those justifiers are keys to her getting people to buy your book.

Hm. There are fourteen primary reasons people use when deciding whether to buy your book. And my sales VP is very interested in how those reasons are displayed in your book. And you want both my sales VP and the eventual reader to be very interested in buying your book.

So, class, what does that mean, in practical terms, for the aspiring author who wants to avoid rejection? Anyone? Anyone? Bueller?

The obvious answer is twofold. First, you should make sure your book offers something that makes spending money on it justifiable to a reader. Second, you should make sure your proposal shows my sales VP why she's justified in spending money to contract your book.

Sounds easy, right? Well, that, dear reader, is your next test.

WHAT YOU CAN DO ABOUT IT...
1. Rate your book in all fourteen areas.

After your manuscript is ready, but before you've written the full proposal section for it, take the list of fourteen "justifiers" above and rate your book in each category. Does your book clearly and emphatically help a reader improve her quality of life? Give yourself an A+ in that category. Does your book miss out on helping a reader beautify his home? Be honest, give yourself an F in that category.

Go through all fourteen justifiers to see where your book's strengths lie—and remember, it's OK for your book to miss out on several justifiers. The important thing is to find at least three or four A+ ratings on your list. Those then become part of the "Reader Benefits" statements you'll include in your proposal (see Reason #34 for more on benefits). When you highlight those benefits of your book in terms of how they motivate readers to buy, you'll get the attention of my sales VP (and my marketing VP as well!).

2. Keep track of why you buy.

For the next three months, keep a record of every book or magazine you buy. Write down the title that you bought, and then in a column next to it, write down one specific reason why you bought it. If it seems to fit into one of the fourteen justifiers categories, fine. If not, write down in your own words what motivated you enough to spend your hard-earned money on it.

After three months, organize your list to reflect which justifiers were most influential on your book-buying decisions. Then ask yourself, "What can I learn about book-buyer motivation from what I see in my own buying habits? And how can I use that information to help me convince others to buy my book?"

3. Read a few good books on consumer behavior.

Sure, this seems like a lot of homework for you when all you really want to do is write a great novel or the next best self-help book, but trust me, it's worth it. Just keep a consumer behavior book on the back of the toilet at home and get that education a few minutes each day. That investment will pay off. If you understand why people buy, you can help explain to a publisher why they'll buy *your* book.

There are many good books on this topic available today, but two that I'd recommend are (obviously) *Why People Buy Things They Don't Need* by Pamela N. Danziger and *Buyology* by Martin Lindstrom.

{ Reason № 66 }

Other Books We've Done Similar to Yours Did Not Sell According to Expectations

In my first acquisitions editor job, I quickly learned the importance of internal comparisons when presenting at a publishing board meeting. Regardless of what type of book I was advocating, somebody on my sales team would *always* ask, "What have we done in the past that's like this book? And how did it sell?"

If I was able to make a favorable comparison ("This is like our XYZ book, which sold about 18,000 copies last year"), then I was in good shape. Ah, but if somebody was able to make an unfavorable comparison ("This sounds a lot like our QRS book, and we just got 2,200 copies of that book returned from bookstores last month!"), I knew I was in trouble.

Believe it or not, this has to do with biology as much as it has to do with psychology. According to neuroscientist Jonah Lehrer, the amygdala is "a brain region that, when excited, evokes negative feelings. Whenever a person thinks about losing something, the amygdala is automatically activated. That's why people hate losses so much."[67]

If your book evokes comparisons to, and memories of, the losses my company incurred on previous books, that excites the amygdala in the mind of my sales VP. After all, he's had to count up those losses—and explain to his boss why we're having to write off that author advance and all those marketing expenses because his sales team didn't sell enough copies of that book.

And so, this is another case where you are (possibly unfairly) judged by the fact that someone you don't know, who came before you at my publishing house, caused our company to lose money on a previous book.

Yeah, some people screw things up for everybody, don't they?

WHAT YOU CAN DO ABOUT IT...

1. Pay attention to what my company sells well.

If you've already done your homework in the areas of market competition and differentiation (see Reasons #45, 46, and 47), then this should be easy for you. You should already know what my company sells that's related to what you're trying to get us to buy. So use that knowledge to point our attention toward the books we've been successful with, and

---

67   Jonah Lehrer, *How We Decide* (New York: Houghton Mifflin Harcourt, 2009), 106.

to let us know we should expect a similar kind of success with your book.

For instance, you could say, "After seeing the success you and your sales team were able to create with ABC book, I am enthusiastic about working with you to repeat that kind of outcome with my new book as well."

The easy way to find these kinds of books is simply to visit a publisher's website and see what backlist books they're still promoting. If a book was released more than a year ago, and it still shows up on the home page or category landing page of the website, it means that book has done well for that company. You can also check book titles on Amazon.com—obviously, anything that ranks higher in a category list is a positive comparison to use. Check your local Walmart or Target store and see what books are on the shelves there—and note which are backlist (more than a year old). Those are books that are doing well for a publisher. And, of course, there are general bestseller lists like *U.S.A Today* and *New York Times* that you can use for comparisons as well.

2. Make positive comparisons with popular books outside my company.

First, let me be clear on this point: *Don't* compare your book's content to the content of a previously successful book. That's simply copycatting someone else's ideas. If you say, "*Freakonomics* was about unique economic theories,

and so is mine!" that just tells me you don't
ideas. (Yawn.)

When making positive comparisons, what you
show why the *audience* that bought a previous book will also
want to buy yours. "*Freakonomics* created a thirst for more
accessible, interesting information about economics. My book
delivers five unexpected principles that will satisfy that thirst
in readers of all ages." You see the difference?

3. Be an artist.

It's been said that an author is simply an artist who paints with
words. If that's true, a lot of writers are still using crayons.

One way to overcome a negative comparison to a previously unsuccessful book is to make your writing such a work
of art that people have a hard time saying yours is like anything
else that came before it. This goes back to issues of quality and
excellence (see Reason #1), but if you can create a work of art
in words, that'll go a long way toward erasing the memory of
past losses in the mind of my sales VP.

As Seth Godin says, "Consumers say that all they want are
cheap commodities. Given the choice, though, most of us,
most of the time, seek out art."[68]

---

68   Seth Godin, *Linchpin* (New York: Portfolio, 2010), 29.

Nothing Similar to Your Book Shows Up on Industry Bestseller Lists

Here's an acronym that's often quoted in bookstores and publishing board meetings: *SMOWS*.

That stands for "Sell More of What's Selling," and it's more than simply a mantra. It's an ingrained business strategy that dictates decisions across the board from my sales VP to my publisher to the bookstores that stock and sell your next book. It's the reason why one successful book on low-fat cooking suddenly produces a glut of low-fat cookbooks in the marketplace, or why a single successful TV series on forensic pathology suddenly multiplies into a dozen shows about people who spend their lives squirming through blood and body fluids to solve crimes.

And SMOWS is why, before your book will pass my publishing board, someone on my sales team will always ask me, "What's this book like in the marketplace?"

This is a tricky question, of course, because what my sales guy is really asking is, "Can I sell more of what's selling with this book?" It's a real, tangible expression of an emotion that psychologists call "loss aversion." That is, it's a deep-seated desire on the part of my sales team to "avoid any option associated with loss"[69] by instead making sure the books they approve (yours included) are somehow associated with success (see Reason #66). In publishing, that means being like a bestseller. Still, if you or I make the mistake of answering that question in a way that makes it seem like we're simply *copycatting* an existing bestseller, that most often spells doom (see Reason #27).

So to avoid rejection in publishing board, our job (i.e., your job in your proposal) is to show the sales team that a) your book is completely unique, and b) your unique book will attract an enormous audience that's already made another book a huge bestseller.

WHAT YOU CAN DO ABOUT IT...

1. Study your industry's bestsellers.

First, find out which bestseller lists are important in your chosen industry.

For instance, the most successful trade books (both nonfiction and fiction) are gauged against one of the major national bestseller lists such as the *New York Times*, or *U.S.A Today*, or *Wall Street Journal*. Specific fiction categories (such as mystery or historical) may benefit from a

---

69   Jonah Lehrer, *How We Decide* (New York: Houghton Mifflin Harcourt, 2009), 76.

Barnes & Noble or Amazon.com list. Religious bestsellers are an industry to themselves, and they show up on either the CBA (Christian Bookseller's Association) list or the ECPA (Evangelical Christian Publishers Association) list. Children's books bestsellers that show up on a list from *Publishers Weekly* carry weight. Industry-specific lists (for example, for textbooks, business books, etc.) are also out there, as well as regional lists (Los Angeles, for instance, or southern states).

The point is, find out which bestseller lists will be important and comparative when it comes time for the sales people at my publishing house to consider your book. Then make sure yours compares favorably to the books on that list.

2. Choose carefully what you identify in your proposal as your book's competition.

As we discussed in Reasons #45 through 47, the market summary and competitive analysis you provide for your book is critical to your book's success during a publishing board discussion. So why not slant that section to favor you and your book? When choosing books for comparative discussion, go ahead and include one or two that are bestsellers on an appropriate list, and play up how your book will attract readers of that book in significant ways. After all, we are known by the quality of our enemies, right?

3. Find a comparative bestseller somewhere— even if it's not a book.

Monopoly has been a bestselling family game for decades. Does your book deliver an experience for families that's similar to the appeal of a game of *Monopoly*? Then heck yeah, you'd better talk about that in your proposal. How about a blockbuster movie? Does your novel deliver to readers an appeal similar to their insatiable hunger for James Cameron's *Avatar*? Well, that's interesting—and my sales VP should know about that as well.

The point is, don't let your book be considered in a void. Find something that has significant sales history—even if it's not a book—and find a way to favorably compare your book to that thing. It could be enough to help my sales team forget to check for other comparable, yet elusive, books on an industry bestseller chart.

{ Reason № 68 }

You Can't Identify Specific Sales Channels That Your Book Will Sell Through

Let me ask you a question: how do you get "there" from "here"?

If you're like most people, you map out a route that will, hopefully, get you from point A to point B in the shortest, straightest way.

Well, in the world of my sales VP, point A is your book, and point B is the buyer who will pay cash money (or credit) for it. And the map my VP uses to get to point B is filled with what we call "sales channels"—the roads of commerce we'll travel to get some coin for your great book.

You're probably already familiar with the superhighways on this map—you know, the Sam's Clubs and Barnes & Noble chain stores. And you probably know those retail roads are clogged with the traffic of books cramming into those places. Your best bet for success, then, is being able to show my sales VP a few other, potentially profitable avenues to take when selling your book.

Let me give you an example of what I

mentioned to you my friend Mikal Keefe

wrote a children's book about a disabled (

chair basketball. As part of his research fo

tacted a wheelchair manufacturer and learned all about the distinctive engineering required to make a child's wheelchair basketball-worthy. At the same time, they learned about his cool, new, affordable kids' book.

Fast-forward a bit, and next thing you know, copies of Mikal's children's book were being included in the pocket of every wheelchair this company rolled off the assembly line. As Mikal told me later, "I had a very happy publisher."

So what about your book? How will it get from point A to point B? Do you know? Have you given it any thought at all? If you're like most writers, you'll just leave that part of the equation to my sales team and hope for the best.

But then again, if you're like most writers, you'll also get rejected.

WHAT YOU CAN DO ABOUT IT...

1. Be aware of typical sales channels—and show how your book will succeed in selling through them.

Here are some of the most common sales channels my sales team are working with every day: "big box" retailers like Sam's Club and Costco; national chain retailers like Barnes &

, Borders, Lifeway Christian Stores, and so on; indepen-
nts (locally owned bookstores); rack jobbers (independent
wholesalers that manage the inventory of other retailers, such
as grocery stores or drugstores); library associations; Internet
retailers and wholesalers; book clubs; school associations;
business associations; charity groups; direct to consumer
(when my publisher bypasses retailers and tries to sell directly
to the reader); and any niche channels on their radar (like the
aforementioned wheelchair manufacturer).

Which of these channels will your book sell through? When
it's time to predict the future sales of your book, my sales VP
will contact his key salespeople working in each of these channels. He'll ask how many copies they estimate they can sell in
their channels, then he'll add up their numbers to get a total
first-year projection in unit sales for your book.

The more channels in which your book can travel, the better it looks in the eyes of my sales VP. And if you can add on
brand-new sales channels my VP hasn't thought of yet? Well,
that's even better.

2. Interview a retail book buyer.

Yes, this is homework. But it should be fun and it will broaden
your understanding of the book industry immensely.

First, create a list of questions that are both sincere and
not stupid. For instance, "What does a book buyer do during
a typical workday?" is a sincere question. "Why doesn't your

company stock my book?" is a stupid one. Limit your questions to between five and eight total, so that you can conduct your interview in about fifteen minutes max.

Next, call the headquarters of your favorite bookstore chain and ask to speak to a secretary in the book buyers' department. Tell the secretary you're doing research for an article for your website or for a report for your writer's group, and ask if one of their buyers would be available for a fifteen-minute interview about his or her job. Then conduct the interview—and apply what you learn!

3. Brainstorm unexpected sales channels for your book.

Of course, in order to be successful in publishing, you're going to have to figure out how to succeed in the traditional sales channels above. However, you can add on success by exploiting unexpected sales channels. So gather a few friends and brainstorm where those channels might be. Is yours a gift book on marriage? Maybe it'd sell in all the wedding chapels in Las Vegas and Atlantic City. Is yours a medieval thriller novel? Maybe it would sell on a medieval fair circuit that thrives during the summer months. You get the idea.

If your nontraditional sales channel can generate 1,000 copies or more in sales, that's something my VP will notice—and may reward.

{ Reason № 69 }

Your Book Costs Too Much to Make

Try this little experiment.

Go to Amazon.com and search in the books category for "greatest song lyrics of today." Are you surprised by the results (or lack of them)? By the fact that Amazon can't even recommend similar searches to find a full book of today's great song lyrics?

I'm not.

Here's why: If you were to publish a book of, say, lyrics of the top one hundred songs in the past ten years, it'd cost you a *fortune*. You'd have to pay a print license fee (akin to a royalty) for every single song for every single copy of the book you printed—whether the book actually sold or not. That kind of project would not only be a pain to compile, it'd cost so much to make that it simply wouldn't be worth the investment.

Similarly, let's say you wanted to publish a 3-D pop-up book with paper glasses attached. Sure, a remarkable few publishers could afford to do that kind of special format book (Disney comes to mind), but for most publishing houses the costs of design and printing would simply be prohibitive. I remember talking with an editor at Simon & Schuster once about a kids' book that had fold-out pages (to create a panorama) instead of bind-in pages. She loved the concept and the author's creative story to go with it...until the printing estimates came in. The book was a great idea, but it simply cost too much to make. Rejection.

What about your book? Does it have particularly expensive content? Does it require special illustrations or tricky design and significant investment in reprint permissions? Does it have to have special format printing or some other unique, but pricey element?

If it does, that's probably a pretty cool book—and it probably will be rejected. Yes, some of those kinds of books do get published—but they are rare. Especially for a writer early in his or her career.

For you, then, a cool-but-pricey production or content concept will probably result in a lot of effort that generates just another rejection letter.

WHAT YOU CAN DO ABOUT IT...
1. Strip away the bells and whistles.
I know one publishing CEO whose mantra is, "People will read content on a napkin, as long as that content is compelling." And he's right. If your content is superb, people will read it regardless of the vehicle it's attached to. So if you're creating a cool

new project and thinking to yourself, "Wouldn't it be cool if this book also did…," then stop and think twice. As they say, the only thing required is what's required. So stick with creating excellent content first, and after you've made yourself into a successful author, you can try adding the bells and whistles later.

2. Be more than a gimmick.

Related to suggestion #1 above, this suggestion is for those of you who are more excited about a movie's special effects than you are about its story.

What you want your book to do is generate repeat readings, to keep bringing people back to your pages time and again. Even the most novel of innovations becomes mundane after a while. (Remember how cool—and pricey—the cell phone was when it first came out in force? Now they are given out for free and left as playthings for little children.) So don't rely on a gimmick to sell your book idea. Gimmicks always get old, especially to a publishing pro who has seen a lot better than what your gimmick can do. Instead, plant your hopes firmly in the garden of your inescapable content and you should do just fine.

3. Be aware of cost-increasers associated with your book.

Full-color art always costs significantly more than two-color or single-color printing, and it practically dictates printing presses from overseas—which increases shipping and warehousing costs as well. Excessive reprint permission fees (for song lyrics or maps or graphics or excerpts from other authors' works) can add up pretty quickly. Special formats for a book (unusual trim size or shape, out-of-the-ordinary binding) also jack up the printing costs for a book.

Pay attention to these kinds of things when shaping your new book product. If you can, eliminate any cost-increasing features that are required to produce the final product of your book. Doing that also eliminates what may later become an obstacle when my sales VP is judging the ROI (return on investment) for your book.

{ Reason № 70 }

You Want Too Much Money

Looking back on it now, I should have just kept my mouth shut. After all, they always say the best negotiators are the ones who speak least, and last.

But what did I know? I was a young whippersnapper, fresh off a string of successes, ready to move and shake and all the other stuff that makes an agent feel more important than he (or she) really is.

I had a new book by a prominent author, and it was superb. Not only was the writing well above average, but it fit so well with reader tastes and current trends I could almost guarantee its success in the marketplace. I felt 25,000 in first-year sales would be easily achieved, and (God willing!) it might even exceed those lofty expectations.

Apparently my opinion was shared, at least in part, by others because three different companies expressed initial interest in publishing. The first publisher contacted me to begin negotiations.

"What kind of advance is your author expecting for this book?" was his question.

Looking back on it now, I should have kept my mouth shut. Or, at best, I should have simply said, "What kind of advance fits with your budget?" and then negotiated from there. Instead I fired off an email: "$15,000 advance."

The publisher quickly thanked me for my time and ended the negotiation. I was able to surmise later that his budget was more in the $2,500 to $5,000 range. And honestly, my author would have taken that. I was the one who got greedy.

The good news is that this book did eventually sell to one of the other publishers interested in it (for a $7,500 advance). The bad news is that I damaged my relationship with that first publisher by demanding too much too fast. Even though I knew his company would likely do a good job creating and selling that book, I also knew his company could never afford to pay a $15,000 advance for it. Yet I demanded that paycheck anyway.

No surprise that publisher routinely rejects everything I send him now. He probably sees my name on the proposal and thinks, "Can't afford this guy. No sense wasting his time and mine."

WHAT YOU CAN DO ABOUT IT...

1. Understand how a royalty advance is calculated.
OK, pay attention, because this can be confusing.

Some people think a royalty advance is a reflection of an author's reputation, or a sign of respect shown to a writer, or a badge of honor to brag about to others in the industry. It's not. It's just an added risk for the publisher that's carefully calculated based on projected income from the first-year sales of a book. There are variations and nuances to this that I can't really cover here, but the basics go something like this:

First, the sales department sets an expected retail price for your book, the standard trade (wholesale) discount, and projected unit sales for the first year (the number of books they think they'll sell). Trade discounts can get a little complicated because publishers also figure the ratio between how many books are expected to sell through bookstores and how many will sell directly to the customer. Still, most wholesale discounts run between 40 percent and 65 percent off the retail price (depending on the size of bulk orders), so when creating a book's initial budget, using a discount somewhere in the middle—say 50 percent—is pretty standard.

Next, to figure your advance, your publisher will predict first-year income by multiplying the retail price by the wholesale discount, and then multiplying that result by the projected first-year unit sales. For instance, the equation for a \$16.99 book with a 10,000 first-year unit sales projection would look like this: $(16.99 \times .5) \times 10{,}000 = \$84{,}950$ first-year income.

Then, your publisher will multiply that predicted first-year income by your royalty percentage rate. If, for instance, yours is a 12 percent net royalty on that \$16.99 book, then their projected *maximum* first-year royalty payment to you would be \$10,194.

That means, under no circumstances will you be offered more than $10,194 as an advance. In reality, you'll probably be offered about half of that—$5,000—simply because all of the publisher's numbers are guesses at this point and it's always wise to hedge one's bets a little bit. (Hey, what if your book only sells 6,000 copies instead of the predicted 10,000?) They might go up to a $7,500 advance if they like your book a lot, but that's where you'll likely top out.

Now, if you've done the math and you know that $7,500 is the top of your publisher's risk threshold, asking for $10,000 or (like I stupidly did) $15,000 as an advance against royalties is simply going to get you yet another rejection.

Dang...and you were so close.

2. Don't expect your writing career to support you.
Sure, someday maybe you'll be able to quit your job and write full time. At least that's the dream, right? But in reality, the only people who do that are a) married to someone who loves them enough to work full time on their behalf, or b) already wealthy enough that they don't need the money they make from writing.

I know one author who has written quite a few books, even briefly placing two of them on a *New York Times* bestseller list. Talented guy, well respected in his genre...and he averages $18,000 a year as a full-time writer. Believe it or not, he's one of the "successful" ones among us!

So don't stare starry-eyed into the great blue beyond of a

writing career and hope that publishing a book or two is the answer to all your financial woes and worries. View it for what it really is for most people: an enjoyable part-time job, something to do alongside a full-time career or in conjunction with a supportive spouse who has a full-time career.

3. Be willing to wait for the back end.

Whenever one of my authors is given the choice between a higher advance with a lower royalty percentage or a lower advance with a higher royalty percentage, I always recommend taking the second option over the first. Sure, a higher advance means more spending money right away, but it almost never pays off on the back end—that is, after the book is out and selling in the market.

If your book is worthwhile and legitimately salable, you want to get a higher percentage of the profits generated when it sells. Not only is that smart business, it also may be something that helps my sales VP feel like he's minimizing the up-front risk on your book. And that could mean a contract for you instead of a rejection letter.

{ Reason № 71 }

Your Novel Is Not a "Romance"

Look, it's not that salespeople in the publishing industry don't work hard. It's just that they don't *like* to work hard. That means they're always looking for something with built-in sales appeal—something that actually sells itself to bookstore buyers and the public at large.

Enter romance novels.

The romance genre of fiction (IMHBAO[70]) is often trite, formulaic, poorly plotted, and occasionally eye-rollingly awful. It's also, by a significant margin, the top-selling genre of fiction. And it's had a lock on that number one spot for decades. Consider these numbers:[71]

- Romance fiction generates about $1.37 billion a year. (Yes, that word was "*billion.*")
- Romance novels outsell mystery and science fiction/

---

70 In My Humble but Accurate Opinion.

71 "Romance Literature Statistics: Overview," Romance Writers of America, www.rwanational.org.

fantasy novels by more than a two-to-one margin. In fact, in a typical year, romance alone sells more than mystery and sci-fi *combined* ($1.37 billion to $1.22 billion).

- As recently as 2008, romance fiction was the "top performing category on the *New York Times*, *U.S.A Today*, and *Publishers Weekly* bestseller lists."

- Seventy-four million people admit to reading at least one romance novel in a year.

So what does all that mean for you? Well, according to publishing industry expert Robert Bly, "Romance gives [a writer] the greatest chance for success."[72] And, alternately, if you're a novelist trying to publish in any genre besides romance, you've already stacked the deck against yourself.

Personally, my version of hell is being locked in an endless maze of romance novels (with country music playing over hidden speakers!), so I avoid romance books whenever possible. And obviously, because I'm biased against the genre itself, I can't make a legitimate judgment as to whether a romance novel is actually good or bad (they all seem bad to me).

But I also know that an overwhelming majority of readers disagree with me on this point—and because of that, my sales VP will also disagree. "We can't sell this book," he'll be thinking. "There's no love story."

And when it's time to vote, he'll vote against your

---

72   Robert Bly, *88 Money-Making Writing Jobs* (Naperville, IL: Sourcebooks, 2009), 247.

proposal (and against me) because he knows your book doesn't appeal to the most fervent fiction buyers out there: romance readers.

WHAT YOU CAN DO ABOUT IT...
1. Switch to romance and pay your dues.

At some point you have to ask yourself, "Am I a novelist? Or am I a [fill in your chosen genre] writer?" If you're dedicated to a specific genre of fiction, then there's not much you can do about this reason for rejection except to write great books that people want to read regardless of genre.

But if you see yourself as a writer first, and your genre as secondary, then you might want to try building your career with a few romance novels to start. That will give you some publishing credits, good experience working in the industry, and—hopefully—some positive sales numbers to hype when it comes time to pitch a non-romance novel to publishers.

This approach worked well for people like Janet Evanovich and Terri Blackstock—good writers tend to excel no matter what genre they pursue. So give it some thought; if you don't mind reading romance, then try writing it. Study the leaders in the field; dissect the formulas used by publishers like Harlequin or Avon. Then dive in! Who knows...you may actually like it.

2. Try to marry your genre with romance.

It's been said that every good story is a love story, and honestly, that's most often true. So if you can't write straight-up, bonnets-n-buggies romance, then think about how you can marry your chosen genre to elements of romance.

Can you highlight the love triangle between your action hero, his best friend, and that pretty redhead forced to go along on their adventures? Does your fantasy character meet a mysterious, green-skinned, magical woman with alluring tendencies? Great—play that up as well.

Generally speaking, if you can add the "R-word" to your genre—for instance, "romantic suspense," "sci-fi romance," "romantic Western," etc.—you can increase your audience appeal. That, in turn, increases the chances that my sales VP will look favorably on your book proposal. So, if it doesn't destroy the integrity of your story, go ahead and romance it up a bit. After all, every great story is a love story, right?

3. Fall in love.

Every genre benefits from some kind of love story. And every book inherently reflects the personality and experiences of its author at the time it was written. So, why not take time to fall in love (or fall in love all over again) when it's time to write a new novel? Woo your husband all over again, just to enjoy the thrill of it. Seduce your wife again, just to remember what it was like to anticipate and articulate your love. Or, if you're single, get out there and find Mr. or Miss Right. Then, when you're in the throes of hormone-addled ecstasy, write your novel.

You won't even have to try to include a romantic element in a book like that. Because it's a part of your daily life already, it will turn up naturally in your manuscript.

And besides, it's nice to be in love. That way, even if your novel never sells, there'll be at least one person who still thinks you're wonderful—and who might even read your book.

{ Reason № 72 }

My Sales Team Is Struggling to Sell Our Current Line of Books

Imagine that you and I spend an entire day at the beach. Good times, huh?

Now imagine that while you are out surfing it up and having a blast, I get sunburned and stung by a jellyfish and a bully kicks sand in my face.

Tomorrow, when you pop over and invite me to join you for a trip to the beach again, I will probably squint miserably into the sunshine peering through your smile and say, "No thanks!" There's no way I want to risk getting burned again.

Sometimes that's what it's like with my sales team, especially if we're facing a time of economic downturn, or corporate layoffs, or just bad annual reviews from our collective bosses. Remember, emotional discouragement affects intellectual outlook. If my sales VP is discouraged by the performance of the books her team is currently struggling with, she's going to be hesitant to expose her team to further failure with anything that's not a slam-dunk, absolute-guaranteed hit.

Now, if you've done your homework (and I really hope you did!), then you're sending me a book that targets the same audience as previous and/or current books we're publishing. That's a correct strategy almost all of the time…but I'm going to be honest and tell you that if the bottom has unexpectedly fallen out of our core market, your new book could fall out with it.

How are you to know that my sales VP has become disillusioned with the types of books we've been publishing because our typical reader hasn't been buying those books lately? Well, you can't know that. But it still may earn you a rejection anyway.

Sorry about that.

WHAT YOU CAN DO ABOUT IT…

1. Deliver a plan for beating a bad publishing economy.

At this point, you should know why people buy books (see Reason #65). You know specific sales channels where your book has good potential (Reason #68). You've worked on building your platform (Reason #33) and identified any "brandwagon" opportunities that'll help sell your book (Reason #55). You've trimmed the costs of producing your book (Reason #69) and even delivered clear, obvious appeal to women with your book (Reason #59). Add to that all the marketing and editorial expertise you've gained, and you should be able to present a proposal that beats any bad economy, right?

So be sure to use that knowledge to tell my sales team exactly why they'll be successful when selling your book—even though some other loser's book on a similar topic hasn't been good enough. Do that, and you can make my sales VP forget the past and look forward to a bright, shiny future with you in it.

2. Stay away from hard-luck cases.

Sorry to say it, but sometimes it's best not to send a book to a publisher—especially if you keep reading about corporate restructures, "right-sizing," quarterly losses in operating income, or even looming bankruptcy possibilities. Your book won't save that kind of company—and they probably won't appreciate your offer to publish anyway.

So don't try to force your book into a hard-luck company. Give it a year or so to see if they're able to rebound first. Then when all their cost-cutting measures of the previous year start to pay off, they'll be more receptive to the new opportunity that your book provides.

3. Subscribe to *Publisher's Lunch*.

If you're not already on their list, go to PublishersMarketplace .com and sign up for the free, daily e-newsletter, *Publisher's Lunch*. (Heck, if you can afford about $20 a month, go ahead and register on their site for the *Lunch Deluxe* newsletter.)

Publisher's Lunch is one of the most reliable, sources for business information about everybody a the publishing industry. If a publisher is struggling, you'll fi out about it here. If a publisher is expanding, you'll find that here too—along with specific editor names and projects currently in production.

The information you gain from regularly reading *Publisher's Lunch* will be invaluable as you try to navigate unpredictable economic times to find the sales team most likely to be excited about your book.

for Rejection • 329

No Real Sequel Potential for Your Book

Megan Tingley, senior vice president and publisher of Little, Brown Books for Young Readers, blames J.K. Rowling and Stephenie Meyer.

> *"Harry Potter and Twilight," she says, "created a market for hardcover series with more complex, substantive storylines where readers could live in the world a bit longer. I think people came to want something different out of their reading experience, and it became more about depth than speed."*[73]

Of course, series have been popular for a long time (*Lord of the Rings* or *Narnia*, anyone?). But recent statistics bear out Tingley's observation of a renewed interest in this publishing strategy. For instance, at the time of the writing of this book, an overwhelming 73 percent of the bestselling juvenile books

---

73 "Now in Hardcover: The Series in 2010," *Publishing Trends* newsletter, PublishingTrends.com (May 2010).

are part of a larger series of books.[74] And, of related in...

91 percent of romance novel readers say they are "likely t...
seek out an author's previously published titles after reading a
novel from an author they like,"[75] while 89 percent of general
readers also say they "make a special effort to look for other
books by the same author."[76]

This potential for series books can play a factor in nonfiction acquisitions (for instance, when pitching this book
to publishers, I also included a few ideas for sequels).
However, not many nonfiction books are first acquired as
series books. Typically, with nonfiction, a publisher wants
to know that a series *could* happen—but isn't terribly interested in making a series until after that first book takes off
in the marketplace.

Fiction, however, is a different story—particularly mystery,
romance, and sci-fi/fantasy novels. When I acquired suspense
novels, I routinely looked for series potential as a part of my
evaluation process. Other editors do the same.

"When we bring an author's proposal or manuscript
to acquisition," says Stephanie Lurie, editorial director of

74 "Now in Hardcover: The Series in 2010," *Publishing Trends* newsletter, PublishingTrends.com (May 2010).

75 "Authors and Readers," *Romance Literature Statistics: Readership
Statistics*, Romance Writers of America, RWANational.org.

76 Zogby, *The Reading and Book Buying Habits of Americans*, a white
paper commission by Random House (May 2008), 9.

Books for Children, "often sales will ask
e, and we'll sign them up as a series from

to say that a single, stand-alone novel can't
sell—of course, they're published every day. But it does say
that, especially for fiction writers, the potential for a series of
successful novels can be an attractive element when my sales
VP takes a look at your proposal.

Something to think about.

WHAT YOU CAN DO ABOUT IT...

1. Think in threes.

I'm speaking mainly to novelists right now. After you've come
up with a great idea and written that "next great American
novel," don't assume your work is all done. Before you send
out your proposal to an agent or an editor, think ahead a bit
and create a short (one page or so) summary for two more
novels that could start a series based on your original book.
Think in terms of a trilogy with continuing characters and/or
unique, continued settings that somehow all tie together.

Include those additional book summaries with your proposal, and point out that you are both willing and able to create this as a series for your publisher, or to at least give that

---

77 "Now in Hardcover: The Series in 2010."

publisher the "option of first refusal"[78] on any additional books based on the original. If your original is strong, the prospect of future series potential will be an attractive selling point for any sales VP.

2. And for nonfiction writers...

It never hurts to also think about future possibilities to capitalize on the unmitigated success of the book you're currently pitching. You don't have to go into as much detail about future books in your series as a fiction writer would, but you should at least come up with two or three possible titles and subtitles for books that could be follow-ups to the original one.

List those in your proposal under a heading like "Series Potential" or "Possible Future Books in a Series." It may not actually help your chances of selling the original book (most nonfiction sells as single-book contracts), but it can't hurt. And it may come in handy as a reference when your book hits a bestseller list after publication.

3. Keep an "ideas" list somewhere on your computer.

Some authors think they have to write fully every idea they dream up. That's not true. I personally have over a hundred

---

78 "Option of first refusal" means you promise not to sell your next book to anybody until giving your current publisher the option of contracting it. Usually that means they get a three-month exclusive look at the next book before you are allowed to show it to anyone else.

unused ideas just sitting around on my computer, waiting to be plucked out and created. This well of unused ideas has become a source of many successes for me (including this book). Imagine if I'd never taken the time to jot these things down?

So, whenever you have an idea for a new book, don't judge it right away. Simply jot yourself a few notes about it and then forget about it. Keep adding to your idea well whenever a new idea pops into your creative little brain. Then, when it's time to think about series-izing your next proposal, go back and re-read some of your forgotten ideas on file. Who knows? There may be something there that adapts well to be book number two or number three in a potential new trilogy.

{ Reason № 74 }

My Sales VP Asked a Spouse/ Friend/Baby-sitter if They Would Buy Your Book, and the Response Was Unenthusiastic

Think about the last book you bought. Why did you decide to spend your hard-earned money on that one? If you're like the majority of Americans, it's because someone close to you recommended it. In fact, three of every five Americans indicate that what makes them "want to buy a book" is a suggestion from a friend or family member.[79]

This makes sense. After all, those closest to us—those we trust—are typically people with similar tastes, people who know us and who have our best interests in mind. Sure, they may miss from time to time with a recommendation, but for the most part these folks are pretty reliable in our lives.

Guess what? My sales VP is one of those people who turns to friends and family when he wants a quality recommendation on a book.

---

79 Zogby, *The Reading and Book Buying Habits of Americans*, a white paper commission by Random House (May 2008), 8.

In fact, my sales VP trusts his wife's opinion—or even his baby-sitter's opinion—more than he trusts the hype you've plastered all over your proposal pages. If my VP gets along with his family (yes, even dragons have families!), and if your book is on his mind after a day at work, he's going to talk about it to his wife and kids. Maybe over the dinner table. Maybe during chores. Maybe when they're between innings at Junior's eighth-grade baseball game. Trust me, the topic will come up.

What's more, if he's on the fence about your proposal—maybe he likes the writing but not the trade channel prospects—he's even more likely to solicit a second opinion from somebody around the house. That puts a lot of power into the opinions of someone only tangentially involved in publishing—or maybe into the hands of someone who doesn't really know the first thing about writing except that she didn't like *Brisingr* as much as she liked *Eragon*.

Still, it happens—and it may be the reason your book is rejected.

WHAT YOU CAN DO ABOUT IT...

1. Assume that quality is your safeguard against unofficial critics.

Truth is, you have no control over whether my sales VP seeks out a second (or third) opinion on your book. Sure, if you've done everything well in your proposal, my VP should be able to vote an unequivocal "yes" without needing extra input. But you and I both know that's often just wishful thinking.

On the other hand, when my sales VP asks his baby-sitter what she thought of your book, enthusiasm for your writing from that person will carry a lot of weight. So take care to write with quality and skill for your intended audience. That, in the end, is your best safeguard against any critic—husband, wife, child, friend, baby-sitter, or anyone.

2. Preempt a similar audience.

If you're writing for women, and my sales VP is a man, he's likely to show your book to his wife as a representative of your audience. So why not do that before he does?

Find a few people who are representative of your reading audience, and solicit their sincere criticism of your work. This works best if your representatives are not your family members, but a few friends is usually fine. Ask for written critiques. Then, when they come in, quote some of the most favorable comments and include them in your proposal under a section titled "What People Are Saying about [Book Title]."

For instance, if your book is for hair stylists, you might quote as follows: "So interesting! I never knew there were so many possibilities in my job before I read [book title]"—Mandi, chief stylist at Kassie's Salon.

3. Relax.

Hey, you can't micromanage everything. If you've honestly done the best job you can on your book and its accompanying proposal, this reason for rejection may just need to be one of those things you just leave up to someone else. No sense worrying too much over what, really, is out of your control, right?

*My Sales Team Asked a Few
Key Book Buyers if They Would
Stock Your Book, and Their
Response Was Unenthusiastic*

This is actually a pretty common practice—and one that's fairly smart on the side of any publisher's sales team.

When I worked in acquisitions for both fiction and nonfiction, there were several occasions when a book I was advocating was put on hold so that members of my sales team could call a few key bookstore buyers to get their opinions. If the buyer at Sam's Club said she'd likely stock the book, that was a good thing. If a buyer at one of the national chains—say Barnes & Noble or Lifeway—said he couldn't see my book on their store's shelves, well, that was pretty difficult to overcome in the publishing board meeting.

The reason for this is simple: money. (Surprised?)

According to a 2009 report from the Association of American Publishers, "trade books" (hardcover and softcover adult and juvenile books that are best suited for sales through bookstore channels) are the number one moneymakers in this industry, accounting for more than $8 billion in net annual sales.[80] This becomes even more significant when you consider that, over the past decade, bookstores have been closing at an alarming pace. In 2000, there were 2,794 bookstore members of the American Bookseller's Association. In 2010, that number had shrunk by almost half, to 1,410.[81]

The 2011 bankruptcy, and subsequent store closings, of Borders bookstore chain makes this statistic even worse—and will cost many writers the opportunity to publish. Consider: Borders might promise to carry five copies of your book in each store, but today there are 250 fewer Borders stores than there were yesterday. That means Borders will be carrying 1,000 fewer copies of your book in their sales channel—and that's enough to turn what could have been a profitable book into one that loses money. Rejection soon follows that kind of forecast. And if Borders says they'll only carry two copies of your book in each store? Well, your chances of publishing have just gone from slim to none.

"Big publishers are primarily interested in 'bookstore books,'" says industry veteran Robert Bly.[82] And he's right. If

---

80 Management Practice, *2009 S1 Report: Estimated Book Publishing Industry Net Sales 2002–2009* (Washington, DC.: Association of American Publishers), 2.

81 "ABA Actually Gains (9) Members for the Year," *Publisher's Lunch* e-newsletter (May 24, 2010).

82 Robert Bly, *88 Money-Making Writing Jobs* (Naperville, IL: Sourcebooks, 2009), 41.

your new book doesn't demand a place on bookstore shelves, chances are good it won't be published at all.

WHAT YOU CAN DO ABOUT IT...

1. Visit a few bookstores to see what's getting the prime shelf space.

"Know your enemy," as they say. Shelf space is definitely limited in the typical bookstore, and that makes it valuable. Yet hundreds of books are still prominently displayed in just about any place that sells books. So your mission, should you decide to accept it, is to find out why those books got the prime spots at Barnes & Noble, or at Borders, or Books-a-Million, or your local independent bookstore.

Visit three or four stores. Try to mix your visits between national chain stores and independent (sole owner) stores. You might even pop into Sam's Club or Costco and see what's going on there. Then make a list of all the qualities you notice about the highlighted books on each store's shelves, and look for identifiable trends across all bookstores—these are obviously elements that appeal to book buyers at these stores.

When you're done, figure out how to position your book so it fits into some of those identified trends. Then when my sales VP asks a book buyer for an opinion about your book, the answer she'll get will be, "Sure we'll stock it—it fits right in with what we're doing at our store!"

2. Use BISAC categories to help make your work bookstore-friendly.

Don't ask me what BISAC stands for—I don't know and I don't care. But the BISAC Subject Headings List is the bookstore industry standard for categorizing books. Created by the Book Industry Study Group, Inc., it's a complicated, detailed, subject-tree-style list that—despite its complexities—is actually fairly easy to use. Every publisher looks to the BISAC list when labeling the category for a book, because just about every bookstore in America organizes its shelves based on the categories here.

When you're getting ready to write up a proposal for your book, go ahead and browse the BISAC Subject Headings List until you find a strong category that fits your book. Then be sure to identify your book as part of that exact category in the materials you send to the publisher. If they're already having trade sales success in that category, they'll be glad to know yours fits in.

Here's the web address for the specific page of the 2010 BISAC Subject Headings List (the last update at the time this book was published): http://www.bisg.org/what-we-do-0-136-bisac-subject-headings-list-major-subjects.php.

3. Emphasize significant non-trade sales options for your book.

The truth is, many books make their money *outside* of trade bookstore sales—through direct-to-consumer efforts, or in professional association channels, and so on. In fact, a book that must rely solely on trade sales is probably going to struggle anyway.

So, in your book's proposal, temper the need for significant sales in the bookstore channels by emphasizing the non-trade channels where you think your book will have success. (See Reason #68 for more on this.)

{ Reason № 76 }

Your Book Failed a Focus Group

In the summer of 1983, editor Sarah Gillespie of United Features Syndicate eagerly signed then-unknown cartoonist Bill Watterson to a development deal for a paltry $1,000. The deal was for Watterson's quirky little comic strip titled *Calvin & Hobbes*.

According to Watterson biographer Nevin Martell, Gillespie and her editorial VP, Dave Hendin, "were under a great deal of pressure from the corporate executives…to bring in higher profits." As a stepping-stone toward that profit goal, and "to determine which strips had the most commercial potential, [parent company] Scripps insisted United use focus groups for their untested comic strips."

And so, Mr. Hendin and Ms. Gillespie dutifully trotted out about a month's worth of *Calvin & Hobbes* cartoons and presented them at several focus groups around the country.

The cartoon failed.

Sarah Gillespie was angry, and appealed to the corporate brass to save Watterson's little creation. But the focus groups' decision was final. Gillespie was told, "F*ck it, we can't take everything." So United Features Syndicate sent Bill Watterson a rejection for *Calvin & Hobbes*.

Almost two years later, Lee Salem at Universal Press Syndicate handed Bill Watterson a contract for his comic strip about a boy and his tiger. The success was immediate and long-lasting. In fact, the first book collection of those strips sold more than one million copies—and every *Calvin & Hobbes* collection after that did the same.

If, like Nevin Martell, you were to ask Sarah Gillespie to explain her company's astonishingly bad decision-making in regard to Bill Watterson, she'd shake her head ruefully and say, "United didn't take *Calvin & Hobbes* because a couple of housewives in Connecticut said, 'It's OK, but we don't get it.'"[83]

The lesson for us today, kids?

If it can happen to Bill Watterson, it can happen to you.

WHAT YOU CAN DO ABOUT IT...

1. Be sure your book includes obvious appeal for your target demographic.

This is covered in more depth in Reasons #5 through 8 earlier in this book, and also in Reason #59, so if you're unsure what I'm talking about here, then go back and re-read those sections.

---

83 Nevin Martell, *Looking for Calvin and Hobbes* (New York: Continuum, 2009), 61–66, 96.

The main idea here is to write in such a way that you can be supremely confident your work actually appeals to your target audience. Then, when a focus group made up of people from your target audience is assembled, your book will have instant appeal that powers it on to publication.

2. Hold your own focus group.

Here's a newsflash for you: Publishers don't hold a copyright on focus grouping. In fact, all you really need to pull one off is a place to meet, a few polite munchables (like pastries and coffee), and six to ten people who fit your target demographic and who are willing to give their opinions on your book. Presto! You've got a focus group.

If you think your book might be susceptible to negative focus group comments (or even if you just want to get a better sense of how your book will be received by the general reader), hold your own focus group right where you live. It'll be best if you leave your closest friends and family out of this focus group, but a cousin you only see on holidays? Sure, include her. A coworker at your spouse's workplace? Why not?

Strip away any author byline (so people won't know they're criticizing you), compile a list of relevant questions (use this book to spark ideas), and make it happen. Afterward, address any concerns that came up, so the next time your book is focus grouped, it'll be ready. You may even consider highlighting positive results from your private focus group in your book's proposal, just to let the sales team know you've been doing their homework for them.

3. Research before you write.

Many "back end" problems in a manuscript are preventable with "front end" considerations. This is difficult for many writers, though. We've been trained to write first, seek opinions later. But—and I speak from experience here—you can avoid many problems by getting as much information up front as possible.

For a while, I was assigned to edit a line of curriculum for children. My first efforts were, well, not great. So my supervisor wisely instituted a new job requirement for me: At least once a month I had to sit in, all day, with a fifth-grade class at a local public school. I resented the assignment, but I wanted to keep my job so I did it for many months. Surprise—by the time I was done, I'd become almost an expert on what worked and didn't work in a fifth-grade classroom. Editing became easier, and my product line became better—actually winning an award and becoming one of the company's bestselling curriculum lines of all time.

So take the lesson here: Invest time up front studying your audience and researching your content. Then, if you are subjected to a focus group's evaluation, you'll likely pass with flying colors.

{ Reason № 77 }

Bottom Line—Not Enough Profit Potential

People who write books are word folks—that's what empowers us to capture ideas and express them well on the printed page.

People who publish books are numbers folks—that's what empowers us all to actually make money from writing.

If you're a word person and all you want to be is a writer, then go ahead! Nothing is stopping you from writing, nothing at all. But if you want to be a *published* writer—if you insist on adding a price tag to your words—then you'd better learn how to think, and talk, like a numbers person.

I told you this at the start of this book, and I think now is the appropriate time to tell it to you again. First, foremost, and always, there is actually only one overarching reason why any book is published—or rejected:

Profit.

That's it, really.

You must understand that, regardless of how much your editor loves your writing, or how enthusiastic the marketing team feels about your book, or even if your book can literally cure the common cold, the bottom line for decision-making in our corporate publishing industry will always be potential for profit from your book.

Every book that goes through a publisher's approval process is primped and prodded and primed with the goal of making it pass the final feasibility report (also called "P&L—profit and loss," "Pro Forma," and "Projected Book Budget"). Every possible expense we can think of has been tossed into that P&L statement, along with any possible way we can see to bring income from your writing. Down at the bottom of that Microsoft Excel report, typically in bold letters that are either red or black, there's a single number that predicts what our ROI (return on investment) will be on your book. If that number shows 50 percent or higher net return in the first year, chances are very good your book will be published. Anything under 50 percent, and your prospects dwindle.

So, if you want to publish, find out how you can manipulate that bottom line percentage on my company's P&L until it makes my numbers people (specifically, my sales VP) smile.

That's the only guaranteed way to avoid getting a rejection letter for your next book.

WHAT YOU CAN DO ABOUT IT...

1. After you've written words, think in numbers.

This takes a forced change in perspective because, if you are any good as a writer, up to this point you've been 100 percent focused on creating a work of art with words. That's good. Essential really, if only because true art is inherently rare and thus infinitely valuable.

But after you've created the art, after you've bled your heart and soul into your manuscript, after you've taken the intangible idea and translated it into actual, physical words, it's time to stop thinking like an artist. It's now time to start thinking like an accountant. To view your spiritual master-piece as merely another commodity to be bought and sold like pork futures or that shovel on sale at your local Ace Hardware store.

What makes your manuscript something that people will *buy*? And how many will buy it? And how much can your pub-lisher realistically charge for it? And how much will it cost to make it? And how will that paper-and-ink commodity add up on the accounting ledger?

Answer those questions well, and you'll make a kindred spirit out of my sales VP—and you'll earn her vote when it's time to make a decision on your book.

2. Find a way to guarantee a certain amount of sales for your book.

Hey, if money is what really matters in publishing, then being able to guarantee sales that make money gets everybody interested. Of course, that's much easier said than done.

People who are best-positioned to do this are those with a built-in demand for what they create. For instance, leaders of an association that will commit ahead of time to buy 1,000 copies or more out of the first print run on their book. Professors at a university that will require their books as textbooks. A public speaking career that enables you to buy and sell a significant number of your own books each year. A writer's own online store that demonstrates significant sales already. A business leader of a national retail chain that can promise all her stores will carry her book. You get the idea.

3. Remove your "fuzzy focus" lenses.

In the end, you must remove the warm, fuzzy feelings you get from writing and instead be determined to face the facts. Coldly determine what factors influence your publisher's profit potential. Position your book's content and market features to highlight profit potential. Propagandize your book's proposal to hammer home that profit potential for the publisher.

If you can do that, you can make pretty much all seventy-seven reasons in this book go away for good.

{ Afterword }

Congratulations.

If you made it to the end of this book without giving up on your writing career, then you are an author with passion and determination. That's a very good thing. If your writing skill and thinking ability match that passion and determination, well, you just might make a mark in this dirty little business of ours.

Before we part ways, there are just a few last things I want to say to you.

First, thank you for reading this book. You are a special person, and I appreciate that you shared your time with me. You rock.

Second, I know I'm a big, arrogant jerk and that reading this book can be both depressing and overwhelming to aspiring writers. I'm sorry for the "big jerk" part of that equation—but not for the rest. You see, if I can talk you out of pursuing a writing career, then you don't belong in publishing, so it's good that you quit now. If this book prompts you to do that, then it's good for both of us.

Of course, if you truly have the soul of a writer, then nothing I said in this book is going to discourage you from pursuing that career anyway. So, if that's the case, you'll be stronger—and more successful—for having learned what's in here. Welcome to publishing. It sucks. You're gonna love it.

Third, I can't help you get published. Sorry. I know, now that we are friends, some of you out there will immediately see me as the agent who will help you get published, and you'll send me your newest masterpiece before turning the last page of this book. But my agency is full—I simply can't add new writers without adding more time to the day. And since I haven't yet figured out how to manipulate the time-space continuum, let me just go ahead and reject your proposal ahead of time and save us both the awkwardness of that future situation.

Are there any exceptions to my current "no new author clients" rule? Well, I guess so. If you are someone I already know, or someone who comes to me with a strong recommendation from an existing Nappaland client, then OK, I'll take a look at your idea. Otherwise, I'm sorry to say the answer is no. (And if you think this doesn't apply to you, then please re-read Reasons #13, 14, and 23.)

Fourth, despite the previous two paragraphs, I really do hope you succeed in publishing. And I hope that *77 Reasons Why Your Book Was Rejected* helps you to do so. After all, that's why I wrote it—to give you an insider's perspective on the way your various book proposals are received after you send them out into the world. And to share a few ideas for how you can overcome the basic mistakes that 99 percent of writers make when pitching a book.

So I hope this book helps you. I really do.

Well, I guess that's it. Again, thanks for reading. May God bless you in your efforts at publishing.

• • •

Mike Nappa

{ Appendix }

Recommended Resources
for Writers

BOOKS

88 Money-Making Writing Jobs by Robert Bly

1,001 Ways to Market Your Books by John Kremer

Be Your Own Literary Agent by Martin Levin

Buyology by Martin Lindstrom

Children's Writer's & Illustrator's Market by Alice Pope

Don't Think Pink by Lisa Johnson and Andrea Learned

Get Known Before the Book Deal by Christina Katz

Guerrilla Marketing for Writers: 100 No-Cost, Low-Cost Weapons for Selling Your Work by Jay Conrad Levinson, Rick Frishman, Michael Larsen, and David L. Hancock

Guide to Literary Agents by Chuck Sambuchino

How We Decide by Jonah Lehrer

Intellectual Property by Roger E. Schechter and John R. Thomas (highly recommended)

Kirsch's Handbook of Publishing Law by Jonathan Kirsch

Law in Plain English for Writers by Leonard D. DuBoff

Literary Marketplace by various editors

MySpace Marketing by Sean Percival

On Writing by Stephen King

Plug Your Book! by Steve Weber

Publicize Your Book! by Jacqueline Deval

Putting Your Passion into Print by Arielle Eckstut and David
    Sterry
Self-Editing for Fiction Writers by Renni Browne and Dave King
Social Media Marketing: An Hour a Day by Dave Evans
*Social Networking Spaces: From Facebook to Twitter and
    Everything In Between* by Todd Kelsey
Telling Lies for Fun and Profit by Lawrence Block (highly
    recommended)
Telling True Stories by Mark Kramer and Wendy Call
The Art & Craft of Writing Christian Fiction by Jeff Gerke
The Art of Styling Sentences by Ann Longknife and K.D. Sullivan
The Book on Writing by Paula LaRocque (highly recommended)
The Copywriter's Handbook by Robert Bly (highly recommended)
The Facebook Era by Clara Shih
The Pocket Wadsworth Handbook by Laurie G. Kirszner and Stephen
    R. Mandell
The Public Domain by Stephen Fishman
*Jeff Herman's Guide to Book Editors, Publishers, and Literary
    Agents* by Jeff Herman
The Writer's Handbook by Barry Turner
Twitter Power 2.0 by Joel Comm
Why People Buy Things They Don't Need by Pamela N. Danziger
Why She Buys by Bridget Brennan
Writer's Market by Robert Lee Brewer

WEBSITES
Amazon.com (online store and book database)
AuthorCentral.Amazon.com (free author promo page on Amazon
    .com online store)
Blogger.com (free blog site)
Bowker.com (publishing industry information source)

ChristinaKatz.com (blog from the author of *Get Known Before the Book Deal*)

Copyright.gov (website of the U.S. Copyright Office)

Facebook.com (social network)

FreeWebsite.com (free website creation)

ForeWordReviews.com (website for *ForeWord Reviews* magazine)

GoDaddy.com (for paid website hosting)

MediaBistro.com (jobs and resources for freelance writers)

MySpace.com (social network)

netvibes.com/somersault#Publishing (Somersault NOW Dashboard—a clearinghouse of publishing-related RSS feeds)

NetworkSolutions.com (for paid website hosting)

Newpages.com/writing-conferences (a clearinghouse of information about current conferences, workshops, retreats, and so on for writers)

Pred-Ed.com ("Preditors & Editors" website, a clearinghouse of information for authors)

PRWeb.com (for book publicity services)

PublicityHound.com (for book publicity ideas)

PublishersMarketplace.com (home of the *Publisher's Lunch* e-newsletter)

PublishersWeekly.com (website of *Publishers Weekly* magazine)

Twitter.com (social network)

TypePad.com (free blog site)

Wix.com (free website creation)

WordPress.com (free blog site)

WriterMag.com (website of *The Writer* magazine)

WritersDigest.com (website of *Writer's Digest* magazine)

Writing.ShawGuides.com (writer's conference information clearinghouse)

Yola.com (free website creation)

MAGAZINES/NEWSLETTERS/CONFERENCES/OTHER

American Society of Journalists and Authors (ASJA) Annual Writers Conference (www.asja.org/wc)

Bookmarks magazine

Colorado Christian Writer's Conference (writehisanswer .com/Colorado)

Firefly: The Complete Series on DVD (just because, you know, this show rocks)

ForeWord Reviews magazine

Frozen Grand Central, www.youtube.com/watch?v=jwMj3PJDxuo (best visual example ever of the power of "product differentiation")

Greater Philly Christian Writer's Conference (writehisanswer .com/Philadelphia)

Indiana University Writers' Conference (indiana.edu/~writecon)

Library Journal magazine

Mount Hermon Writer's Conference (mounthermon.com)

New York Review of Books magazine

New York Writer's Workshop & Pitch Conferences (newyorkwritersworkshop.com)

Poet's and Writer's Magazine

Publisher's Lunch newsletter (available at PublishersMarketplace .com)

Publishers Weekly magazine

PW Daily newsletter (available at PublishersWeekly.com)

San Francisco Writer's Conference (sfwriters.org)

The Writer magazine

World Literature Today magazine

Write From the Heart Seminars (HalZinaBennett.com)

Writer's Digest magazine

Writer's Journal

Writers Studio at UCLA Extension (uclaextension.edu/writers)

{ Acknowledgments }

I am indebted to a great many people for their encouragement and support.

Thanks to Steve Parolini, my first (and still the best) mentor in the business of publishing. Thanks also to Peter Lynch, the absolute visionary who first saw the potential for this book. Wow, Peter, you look great today, by the way. Have you lost weight? Been working out? Niiice. (Note: See, kids, it always pays to suck up to your editor.) Thanks also to Kelly Bale, whose thoughtful comments and words of encouragement actually made it pleasant to work through the editorial process with a book.

Grateful thanks to my wife, who shared some of her stories and advice with me, even though I get to take full credit for them by including them in this book. (Wow, Amy, you look great today…etc.)

Thanks to Chuck Sambuchino, Chip MacGregor, Marlene Bagnull, and Robert Bly for your thoughtful comments and generous support for this book. Remind me someday that I owe you a favor.

And thanks especially to God, for creating words in the first place. My world would be a silent, desolate place without you.

Best to all!

Mike

{ About the Author }

Mike Nappa is an award-winning editor, a professional marketing copywriter, and chief literary agent at Nappaland Literary Agency. He's also an accomplished author with more than a million copies of his books in print. Plus, he still reads comic books just for fun. So, you know, he's got that going for him. Learn more about Mike at www.MikeNappa.com.